THEOLOGY
OUT OF THE GHETTO

THEOLOGY
OUT OF THE GHETTO

A NEW TESTAMENT EXEGETICAL STUDY
CONCERNING
RELIGIOUS EXCLUSIVENESS

BY

HENDRIKUS BOERS

LEIDEN
E. J. BRILL
1971

To Herbert and Gertraude Braun

TABLE OF CONTENTS

Part two

THE CLAIM OF ABSOLUTENESS IN THE CHRISTOLOGY OF THE NEW TESTAMENT

PREFACE

> "Thought does not stand still. Continually working
> forward, beyond itself, it changes the thinker."
> Paul Natorp, *Platons Ideenlehre*

This study is less a confrontation with New Testament texts than an attempt to re-experience what occurred in these texts. A fundamental conviction of the study is that a text is not so much a product of thought, but a reproduction of a thought process, in so far as it is not itself a written thinking process. And the thinker is not the subject, but the predicate of a thinking process. This is what I understand to be the intention of the above quotation from Natorp, but it was already recognized by Socrates in his opposition to the Sophist subjectivism and has remained a fundamental problem of philosophy ever since. Thus, ultimately, we must come to ask, not only what the author of a text intended, but what happened to him in the writing of the text.

In this study, the question is asked first in connection with the ministry of Jesus. In this case it is difficult since we have no actual text of Jesus, but are dependent on the early Christian tradition which retains nothing in the original form about him. Nevertheless, it appeared necessary to at least try and recover something of that which occurred in his ministry, and the effort does not seem to have been altogether fruitless. A firmer basis was available in the case of Mt. 25 : 31–46 and Rom. 4. In these cases it is not the preliminary establishment of what the texts say which really concerns us, even if the detailed work in this regard could not be spared, but what happened to the authors in the "writing" of these texts.

But that is only one level of what is intended in this study. Even more important is the hope that it can win the reader for that which happened in these texts. The fundamental conviction of the study, thus, also seeks realization as its ultimate purpose, namely, that the reader should experience himself as the predicate and not subject of his thinking, i.e., in as far as the argument proceeds validly he should find it necessary to think in a particular way, as determined by the argument, and not as he would prefer his thinking to proceed. This is what happened to Paul in Rom. 4 where he succumbed as the subject of his own thinking in Christ, to become the predicate of a thinking process which broke him free from the limits set by the confession of Christ, even if this may have been only short-lived. This breaking of the limits set to thought by the confession of Christ, does not have to mean a contradiction of what is thought within these limits, but it allows thought its freedom by forcing the thinker who tries to subject thinking to himself, to surrender this resistance to the freedom of thought and become its predicate. The resistance to thought is based on the absolutizing of a particular experience in which the thinker asserts himself as the subject of his thinking, thus limiting the thinking process. Only by allowing himself to be the predicate of thought is he free to think.

This liberation is needed in theology as much as it is needed in most other disciplines—no less and no more—and this study is an attempt to contribute to such a liberation of thought. The interpretation of New Testament texts may be one of the most appropriate ways of achieving this in theology, since the New Testament faith is the original basis for subjective thinking in Christian theology.

There are a number of persons not mentioned in this book to whom I am indebted for what may have been the most important factor in its writing, namely, the atmosphere in which it became a reality. This atmosphere was produced by the community of, on the one hand, the students in my courses with their continual probing, and, on the other hand, the group of colleagues and past colleagues at Emory University, who met frequently, as we still do, for the sake of critical inquiry: Thomas Altizer, William Beardslee, Martin Buss, Manfred Hoffmann, William Mallard, Theodore Runyon, Jack Sanders and Theodore Weber. I must add to this as a major factor the continual critical interest of my wife, Ida. The manuscript benefited considerably from the suggestions, after careful reading, made by Jack Sanders, William Mallard, William A. Beardslee and Hans Dieter Betz.

The work was completed during the first months of my leave of absence in Bonn, Germany, in 1968/1969, which was made possible by a grant from the American Association of Theological Schools, and a travel grant from the Emory University Research Committee. I thank these institutions for their support.

A word of special thanks goes to Mrs. Frances Pound, who performed more than the usual duties in typing the manuscript, and to

the graduate students James Scott, William Rich and Wayne San-
difer for assisting with the manuscript in a variety of ways.

This book could not have been written without the benefit of the
work of Herbert Braun. By dedicating it to him and his wife,
Gertraude, I wish to express my appreciation for this, but even more
for their allowing me to participate with them in the freedom which
is so characteristic of their existence.

THE PROBLEM

There is a strong awareness of the need to take the world seriously as a partner in dialogue in much of contemporary theology. This is not only evident in those theological writings in which particularly the influence of Dietrich Bonhoeffer[1] and Friedrich Gogarten[2] frequently comes to play, but is also witnessed to as an existential concern of the Christian community itself by the events surrounding Vatican II, which concern not only the Roman Catholic Church, but the entire Christian community—even when there is reaction against it.

However, if there is to be a real dialogue, i.e., if the relationship of Christianity to the world is not to become a monologue in which the attempt is (unintentionally?) made to reduce the role of the world to that of an audience, then the Christian claim that a true realization of man in the world is possible only in Christ cannot be maintained. Otherwise this can only result in the world losing interest, and, having been prevented from active participation in the dialogue, ceasing to participate passively as well, placing Christianity back in its ghetto, speaking to itself.

This problem was stated very clearly by Fritz Buri[3] in his criticism of Bultmann, who, according to Buri, breaks up the fundamental formal association with the philosophers Wilhelm Kamlah and Martin Heidegger "when, against the philosophical self-understanding, he

---

[1] Dietrich Bonhoeffer, *Widerstand und Ergebung*, München: Chr. Kaiser Verlag, 1951; now also as Siebenstern-Taschenbuch 1; Eng. tr., *Letters and Papers From Prison*, Fontana Books, 1959. Cf., particularly Gerhard Ebeling, "Die 'nicht-religiöse Interpretation biblischer Begriffe'," *Zeitschrift für Theologie und Kirche* 52 (1955), pp. 296–360, and also in *Die mündige Welt*, II, München 1956, pp. 12–73; now in *Wort und Glaube*, Tübingen: J. C. B. Mohr (Paul Siebeck), 1960, pp. 90–160; Eng. tr. by James W. Leitch, "The 'Non-religious Interpretation of Biblical Concepts'," *Word and Faith*, Philadelphia: Fortress Press, 1963, pp. 98–161.

[2] Friedrich Gogarten, *Der Mensch zwischen Gott und Welt*, 1st. ed., Heidelberg: Verlag Lambert Schneider, 1952, subsequent eds., Stuttgart: Friedrich Vorwerk Verlag, 1956ff.; *Verhängnis und Hoffnung der Neuzeit*, Stuttgart: Friedrich Vorwerk Verlag, 1953; now also as Siebenstern-Taschenbuch 72.

[3] Fritz Buri, "Entmythologisierung oder Entkerygmatisierung der Theologie," *Kerygma und Mythos*, edited by H.-W. Bartsch, Hamburg-Volksdorf: Herbert Reich, 1952 (abbreviated *KuM.* below), vol. 2, pp. 85–101.

suddenly appeals to the event of the salvation of God in Christ as the
basis for the realization of the Christian self-understanding. With
that he ... breaks off the possibility of a conversation of the theolo-
gian with the philosopher ..."[1] The question is, of course, whether
Christianity can surrender this claim, and, if it can do so, how this
can be done without Christianity losing its identity.

The problem was also brought into focus by Schubert Ogden's
criticism of Bultmann's insistence that the realization of Christian
existence is dependent upon the particular historical event of Jesus
of Nazareth. Ogden's main *theological* argument is that Bultmann's
distinction between a *possibility in principle* which natural man has
to realize authentic existence without Christ, and the *possibility in
fact* which he does not have without Christ, is inconsistent.[2] Briefly
stated Ogden's argument is: "If Christian existence is a possibility
belonging to man *qua* man, and so is something for which he is
always responsible—and this is clearly what Bultmann wants to
affirm when he says it is a 'possibility in principle'—then, in this
case at least, the distinction between 'possibility in principle' and
'possibility in fact' is vacuous,"[3] because: "Unless such existence is a
'possibility in fact' as well as a 'possibility in principle,' it cannot be
a possibility that man is accountable for realizing—although this,
ex hypothesi, is exactly what it is."[4]

Ogden's argument is altogether consistent and cannot be answered by denying that the distinction between a "possibility in
fact" and a "possibility in principle" is vacuous, as is suggested by
Thomas C. Oden.[5] His attempt to disqualify Ogden's objection does

---

[1] Buri, *op. cit.*, p. 91, cf. Rudolf Bultmann, "Neues Testament und Mythologie," *KuM.*, vol. 1, 1st. ed. 1948, pp. 36–41; subs. eds. 1951ff., pp. 33–38;
Eng. tr. by R. H. Fuller, *Kerygma and Myth*, London: SPCK., 1957, pp. 25–30.
   Buri suggested that a carrying through of Bultmann's program calls for
a dekerygmatizing, not a demythologizing of the New Testament (*op. cit.*,
pp. 96–101), but subsequently rejected the term "dekerygmatize" (cf. *Dog-
matik als Selbstverständnis des christlichen Glaubens, Erster Teil: Vernunft und
Offenbarung*, Bern: Verlag Paul Haupt, and Tübingen: Katzmann-Verlag
K. G., 1956, p. 3), suggesting now that what is required "is rather an existential restatement that will permit the kerygma really to come into its own."
(According to Schubert Ogden, *Christ Without Myth*, New York: Harper and
Brothers, 1961, p. 139, note 16, referring to Buri's *Weg des Glaubens*, Münich:
Ernst Reinhardt Verlag, 1958).
   [2] *Op. cit.*, pp. 117–125.
   [3] *Op. cit.*, p. 118.
   [4] *Ad loc.*
   [5] "The alleged structural inconsistency in Bultmann," *The Journal of
Religion* 44, 1964, pp. 193–200.

not really affect the latter's point. Oden suggests three steps in answering Odgen. The first step, according to which "the self-assertiveness which makes (man) think he can achieve authentic life on his own initiative is precisely what prevents him from achieving it,"[1] only suggests why man in fact does not realize the possibility which he may in fact have. The second step is a reference to Reinhold Niebuhr's "ingenious formula" that "sin is inevitable but not necessary"[2] which does not affect Ogden's argument as he has not interested himself in this part of his reasoning in whether man realizes his possibility or not, but whether he has a real possibility for which he can be held responsible. Niebuhr's formula, according to which sin is *not necessary*, in fact confirms that it is a real possibility. In the third step Oden criticizes Ogden for speaking of man as an "isolated individual, not humanity as a whole," and then argues that individual self-realization is not possible because "everyone is responsible for sharing, perpetuating and elaborating the whole history of human estrangement."[3] With this Oden in fact denies that man has the possibility of self-realization. But this would then also apply to Christian authentic existence, which the believer would not be able to realize, unless Christ, as a gnostic redeemer, calls him out of his participation "in humanity as a whole."

The latter possibility is indeed suggested by the Fourth Gospel, and the denial that the realization of Christian existence is a (present) possibility, represents the point of view of Paul (cf. Phil. 3 : 12)—if one can appropriately call salvation according to Paul, authentic existence. According to him the believer participates in salvation, i.e., in Christ, in the present only in hope (cf. the future *esometha* in Rom. 6 : 5; also Rom. 8 : 24f.), which means a proleptic participation in what was still future, and thus not yet a reality—or even a possibility—in present human existence, but for which the believer now has the Spirit as *arabōn*, that which gives the full assurance that it will be a future reality (II Cor. 5 : 5, cf. Rom. 8 : 26f.), after the parousia of Christ (cf. I Cor. 15 : 22f.).[4]

However, it may be asked in connection with Ogden's argument whether the phrases "possibility in fact" and "possibility in prin-

---

[1] *Op. cit.*, p. 197.
[2] *Ad loc.*
[3] *Op. cit.*, p. 198.
[4] Cf. in this regard my article on "Apocalyptic eschatology in I Corinthians 15," *Interpretation* 21 (1967), pp. 50–65.

ciple" adequately reproduce what Bultmann intended when he spoke of the distinction between "eine prinzipielle Möglichkeit" and "eine faktische" in the relevant statements: "(Die Philosophie) hält eine prinzipielle Möglichkeit schon für eine faktische. Nach der Meinung des Neuen Testaments hat der Mensch die faktische Möglichkeit verloren ..."[1] One may best translate this as follows: "Philosophy holds a fundamental possibility to be already a factual one. According to the New Testament man has lost the factual possibility..."

What Bultmann means is that, according to the New Testament, although man has the possibility of authenticity as a basic element in the structure of his existence, he has lost the possibility of realizing it, because he has lost control over his own destiny, and it is only in response to the proclamation of Christ that he is freed from this loss of control. Man as man is still responsible for the realization of his authenticity because he alone can realize it, and as a man he remains a being who is called upon to realize it, even though in fact he has lost the possibility to do so until he regains it in response to the proclamation of Christ. Bultmann can indeed support himself very well for this on Paul—provided "righteousness" is used instead of the questionable "authentic existence" as a designation for salvation in Paul.

Thus in Rom. 1 : 18–3 : 26 Paul argues that although man had the possibility of knowing God, i.e., God's righteousness as the only source of his own righteousness, he lost this possibility. The purpose of 1 : 18–3 : 20 is to prove that no man is capable of finding righteousness, except in Christ (3 : 20–24). Paul first argues that because of their sinfulness, the gentiles were given over to the power of sin (1 : 18–32); then, that the person who is capable of recognizing the sinfulness of the gentiles is thereby not freed from the judgment (2 : 1–11), because Jews and gentiles in fact have a similar situation before the Law (2 : 12–29); and finally, after having argued that God's righteousness cannot be doubted (3 : 1–8), he deals the decisive blow by pointing out that Jews as well as gentiles, i.e., all of mankind, stand condemned by the Law (3 : 9–20, cf. verses 22c–23). When Paul says in 3 : 20 that "through the works of the Law no man is justified before (God)," he means that man has lost the possibility of righteousness for which he is responsible. Unless man

---

[1] *KuM*. I, 1st ed., p. 39; subs. eds. p. 37; Eng. tr., p. 29.

is responsible to the demand of the Law, he could not be subject to that which the Law announces (cf. 3 : 19), namely, that he is incapable of obedience (3 : 20, cf. verses 9–18). The problem, thus, cannot be that Bultmann's distinction, and his insistence that man has lost the factual possibility of obedience which he can only regain in response to the proclamation of Christ, is not true to the New Testament. His insistence is apparently a valid expression of what is the *typical* claim of the New Testament.[1]

If there is a difficulty here, it is with the New Testament, and not one for which Bultmann ultimately can be held responsible. And if we find it necessary to question this claim, our argument has to be with the New Testament. This is precisely what we intend to do below, and in the following way: First, by showing that in the teaching of Jesus no such claim is made; that such a claim is in fact excluded; and secondly, that, although the claim of exclusiveness is what characterizes the New Testament Christology, there are instances in the New Testament itself where this claim is contradicted, e.g., in the description of the last judgment in Mt. 25 : 31–46, and in Paul's reference to Abraham as the example who is followed in the Christian response in faith in Rom. 4. Both are passages to which Ogden correctly refers.[2]

Even if it is true that neither the ministry of Jesus (which has to be recovered from the synoptic gospels) nor the above-mentioned contradictions of the Christian claim of exclusiveness is representative of the intention of the New Testament, they do appear to offer the only possible basis on which a dialogue between Christianity and the world could sensibly take place—except, of course, for the fact that the New Testament could be studied most beneficially as a collection of documents of the Hellenistic era. It is with these uncharacteristic features of the New Testament that we are to be concerned in this study.

---

[1] So Bultmann himself, in his review of "Christ without Myth. By Schubert M. Ogden," *Journal of Religion*, 42 (1962), pp. 225–227, esp. p. 226b.
[2] *Op. cit.*, pp. 143f., and 154f.

PART ONE

THE TEACHING OF JESUS

CHAPTER ONE

THE FUNCTION OF THE PARABLES
IN THE MINISTRY OF JESUS

A. The Three Conceptions of the Parables in Mark 4

Chapter 4 of Mark's gospel reveals most clearly the difficulties encountered by primitive Christians in connection with the understanding of the parables of Jesus, and can serve very well to recover an understanding of their original function in his ministry by distinguishing it from the subsequent understanding of the church. This chapter manifests the typical tensions in the gospel which resulted from the fact that the evangelist collected diverse primitive Christian traditions without completely reconciling them —probably because he did not really try to do so. These tensions become all the more apparent when one recognizes that Matthew was already aware of them, and with typical editorial skill rounded off the rough edges with as little possible alteration of his sources—in this case Marks' gospel. For the sake of clarity the relevant sections are given in parallel.

Mark (4 : 10–13, 33–34)	*Matthew (13 : 10–15, 18, 34–35)*
10 And when they were alone, those who were around him with the twelve asked him (concerning) the parables.	10 And having come (to him) the disciples said to him: Why do you speak to them in parables?
11 And he said to them: To you the mystery of the Kingdom of God has been given: To them who are outside everything comes in parables.	11 And he, replying, said: To you it is given to know the mysteries of the Kingdom of the heavens: To them it is not given.
	12 For whoever has, to him will be given, and he will have in abundance, but whoever does not have, also what he has will be taken from him.
	13 For this reason I speak to them in parables, for seeing they do not see, and hearing they do not hear nor understand. And to them
	14 is fulfilled the prophecy of Isaiah

¹² In order that they will look keenly, and not see, and listen keenly and not understand

lest they turn around and it be forgiven them.
¹³ And he says to them: Do you not understand this parable, and how will you understand all the parables?
³³ And with all such parables he spoke the word to them, as they were capable of understanding
³⁴ (lit. 'hearing'). And without parables he did not speak to them, but in privacy he solved all of them for his disciples.

which says: Keenly you will listen, but not understand, and ¹⁵ keenly look, but not see. Because the heart of this people has become hardened, and their ears hard of hearing, and they have closed their eyes, lest they see with their eyes, and with their ears they hear, and with their heart they understand, and turn around and I will heal them.
¹⁸ You thus, heard the parable of the sower.
³⁴ All of this Jesus said to the crowds in parables,

and without parables he said nothing to them.

³⁵ So that the word of the prophet is fulfilled, which says: I will open my mouth in parables. I will utter what has been hidden since creation.

Mark reproduced the following three distinct conceptions of the parables:

1. Jesus told the parables in order to prevent the crowds from understanding his proclamation, in contrast with his disciples to whom the "mystery" of the Kingdom had been given (Mk. 4 : 11f.). 2. The parables were allegories in normal need of solution in order to lay bare their deeper meanings (Mk. 4 : 13ff., 4 : 34). 3. Jesus told parables as a concession to the limited ability of understanding of his hearers. In this case their meanings were evident to the ordinary hearer from the beginning (Mk. 4 : 33). These three conceptions need further discussion.

1. *Jesus told the parables to prevent the crowds from understanding his proclamation, in contrast with the disciples to whom the "mystery" of the Kingdom of God had been given.* (Mk. 4 : 11f.)[1]

Support for this concept of the parables was found in Is. 6 : 9f.,

---

[1] For the history of the interpretation of Mk. 4 : 11, cf. Appendix A, below.

quoted in verse 12, which was understood to have been a prophecy of the resulting lack of understanding of the crowds.[1] In this case the parables were apparently understood to have had no positive function at all. After their original simple meaning was no longer understood,[2] the followers of Jesus themselves were apparently at first mystified by what they could have meant. At this stage the allegorical meanings of the parables had not yet been discovered.[3] In our verses (4 : 11f.) one should not understand the mystery of the Kingdom of God to have been communicated by means of the parables.[4] The parables were intended solely to prevent those outside from understanding the proclamation of Jesus, which does not mean, however, that they did not conceal references to the Kingdom,[5] but these the hearers were not intended to grasp.[6] The mystery of the

---

[1] So, e.g., Adolf Jülicher, *Die Gleichnisse Jesu*, 2 vols., Freiburg i.B., Leipzig und Tübingen: J. C. B. Mohr (Paul Siebeck), 1899, 2nd. 1910, reprint of the 2nd ed., Darmstadt: Wissenschaftliche Buchgesellschaft, 1963 (references are to the latter), p. 122; Günter Bornkamm, "*mystērion*," *Theologisches Wörterbuch zum Neuen Testament* (abbreviated *ThWb* below), Vol. IV, pp. 823f.; Eng. tr. by G. W. Bromiley, *Theological Dictionary of the New Testament*, Vol. IV, pp. 817f., also *Jesus von Nazareth*, p. 183, note 11; Eng. tr. by Irene and Fraser McLuskey with James M. Robinson, *Jesus of Nazareth*, p. 201, note 11. Also Wilhelm Wilkens, "Die Redaktion des Gleichniskapitels Mark 4 durch Matth.," *Theologische Zeitschrift*, 20 (1964), pp. 311f., cf. p. 311, footnote 28, and Dan Otto Via, *The Parables*, Philadelphia: Fortress Press, 1967, pp. 8f. This interpretation is not accepted, among others, by Ernst Lohmeyer, *Das Evangelium des Markus*, *Kritisch-exegetischer Kommentar über das Neue Testament*, Göttingen: Vandenhoeck und Ruprecht, 11th ed., 1951, p. 84, Joachim Jeremias, *Die Gleichnisse Jesu*, Zürich: Zwingli-Verlag, 1947; 4th ed., Göttingen: Vandenhoeck und Ruprecht, 1956; 6th ed., 1962 (references will be to the latter two, the former of them in parentheses, except where separate reference is made), pp. (9, 11), 11f., 13; Eng. tr. by S. H. Hooke from the 6th ed., *The Parables of Jesu*, New York: Charles Scribner's Sons, 1963, pp. 15, 17; Willi Marxsen, "Redaktionsgeschichtliche Erklärung der sogenannten Parabeltheorie des Markus," *Zeitschrift für Theologie und Kirche*, 52 (1955), p. 269; and James M. Robinson, *Das Geschichtsverständnis des Markus-Evangeliums*, Zürich: Zwingli-Verlag, 1956 (abbreviated *Geschichtsverständnis* below), p. 72, footnote 33.
For a discussion of the function of Is. 6 : 9f. in Mk. 4 : 12 and its parallels, cf. below, Appendix B.
[2] Cf. Section 3, below.
[3] Cf. Section 2, below.
[4] So Jülicher, *op. cit.*, p. 124; cf. William Wrede, *Das Messiasgeheimnis in den Evangelien*, 1st ed., 1901; 3rd ed., Göttingen: Vandenhoeck und Ruprecht, 1963 (references are to the latter), pp. 55–57; Bornkamm, *mystērion*, p. 824; Wilkens, *op. cit.*, pp. 308f., 310f.
[5] Jülicher, *ad loc.*, Bornkamm, *ad loc.*, cf. Wrede, *op. cit.*, pp. 59, 64.
[6] That this was completely senseless was recognized by Wrede, cf. *op. cit.*, p. 61.

Kingdom of God was understood to have been communicated in some other way to the disciples.[1]

That this was not Mark's own understanding of the parables, and these verses, thus, also not his formulation,[2] is indicated by the fact that the parables are frequently interpreted in his gospel in a way which indicates that these interpretations were the true fulfillment of their purpose, e.g., in 4 : 13ff., cf. 34. The disciples are even reprimanded for not grasping the deeper allegorical meaning of the parables in verse 13c. Jülicher resolved this tension in Mark between the understanding that the parables were intended to conceal, and the other that they had a recognizable allegorical meaning by suggesting that since "the disciples also heard all the speeches of Jesus, he naturally directed his parables to them as well. They could not stand around him fruitlessly ..."[3] The hidden meaning which was concealed from the crowds was disclosed to the disciples in private. However, this cannot be regarded as more than an attempt to reconcile the contradictory conceptions of the parables (in Mark).

And if Mk. 4 : 11f. does not give expression to Mark's own understanding of the parables, then these verses also cannot be regarded as originally an expression of the Messianic secret idea of Mark, as has been suggested by Wrede.[4] Nonetheless, Mark may have understood these verses in the sense of the Messianic secret, i.e., of the disclosure of the Messiahship of Jesus to only an intimate few (cf., e.g., 9 : 9). Mark apparently introduced the tradition of verses 11f. between the question of the disciples concerning the parable of the sower which Jesus had just told (verse 10), and the interpretation of that parable (verses 13ff.), which evidently is the

---

[1] Jülicher, *ad loc.*

[2] So Marxsen, *op. cit.*, pp. 261, 264, footnote 1; also Jeremias, *op. cit.*, pp. (8, cf. 11f.), 10, cf. 14; Eng. tr., pp. 14, 17f., who, however, considers it as an authentic saying.

[3] *Op. cit.*, p. 124, cf. Marxsen, *op. cit.*, pp. 256f.

[4] *Op. cit.*, pp. 58, 63f. For a variation on Wrede's view, cf. Marxen, *op. cit.*, pp. 270f. These verses do express Mark's messianic secret motif, but this motif should not be understood as Mark's attempt to reconcile an earlier non-messianic understanding of the life of Jesus. "The motif rather has its 'Sitz im Leben' in the situation of the evangelist. *Now* is the time of the messianic secret, in the proclamation! Its content is the *mystērion*, which is revealed to the congregation, but remains a riddle to those outside." (*op. cit.*, p. 270; cf. also p. 267: "The work of redaction should rather be interpreted strictly from the present of the evangelist.").

real answer to the question of the disciples.[1] This is clearly indicated by the question of Jesus in verse 13: "Do you not know (i.e., comprehend) this parable ...?" This question clearly shows that it was a single parable about which the disciples inquired. Mark may have been aware of the difficulty of the double reply, and may have tried to soften it with the addition of "and how will you understand all the parables," to the question of Jesus.[2] That the understanding of the parables which was implied in verses 13ff. contradicted that of the tradition of verses 11f., was something of which Mark apparently was not aware. He probably understood the latter in terms of the former.

As could be expected, the contradiction did not slip past Matthew, whose manner of handling Mk. 4 : 11f. lends support to the interpretation which we have proposed for these verses. Matthew apparently understood the saying in a sense similar to that which we have suggested, but did not believe that this could have been the original meaning as it was contradicted by the subsequent interpretation of the parables which was given to the disciples, e.g., in Mk. 4 : 14–20 (cf. also verse 34b). In order to remove the contradiction he eliminated the reference to the parables, which stood in contrast to the disclosure of the mystery of the Kingdom to the disciples in his source (Mark) by simply stating that to them, i.e., to the crowds, it was not given. In this way he eliminated the contradiction without departing too greatly from the letter of his source. This applies to the second part of the verse only, not to the first, where Matthew's version, which is verbally identical with that of Luke except for Matthew's additional *hoti*, calls for a different explanation, namely, that it was due to the influence of an earlier form of the saying of Matthew and of Luke,[3] but which does not need to concern us here.

---

[1] So Jeremias, *op. cit.*, pp. (7f.), 10; Eng. tr., p. 14.

[2] Marxsen, *op. cit.*, pp. 260f., cf. 268f.

Luke has the question of the disciples in the singular, i.e., of "this (single) parable," and it may be tempting to find in it support for the more primitive original singular. However, there is no indication that he in fact did know the earlier form. It appears more probable that he altered the Markan version to the singular with specific reference to "this parable" in order to prepare his readers for the parable of the sower which was to follow. Note that in 8 : 11 he also has "this parable."

[3] Cf. Appendix C, on the parallels of Mk. 4 : 11, below.

Thus he also changed the Markan understanding of the quotation from Is. 6 : 9f. Instead of understanding it as a prophecy of the confusion produced, *and intended*, by the parables in the Markan tradition, Matthew took it as an expression of the unwillingness of the crowds to respond positively to the teaching of Jesus. He achieved this by altering Mark's *hina* = "in order that" into a *hoti* = "since, because."[1] Thus, according to Matthew, whatever understanding the crowds may have had, was removed as a result of their hardness of heart, whereas those who responded positively found it all the easier to understand the parables (Mt. 13 : 12). Matthew, and also Mark, had an understanding of the parables similar to the second conception of the parables in Mark's tradition, to which we now direct our attention.

2. *The parables are allegories in need of a solution which lays bare their deeper theological meaning.* (Mk. 4 : 13ff., 4 : 34)

In Mk. 4 : 13ff. an allegorical interpretation is given as solution of the parable of the sower. The understanding is apparently that the actual intention of the parable is fulfilled with this interpretation. This is clearly contrary to the original sense of verses 11f., according to which the parables were intended as a means of concealing the secret of the Kingdom from outsiders.

In verse 13 the disciples are reprimanded for not being able to understand the parable of the sower. This may be a formulation of Mark with which he tried to soften the difficulty of the double reply of Jesus to the question of the disciples which resulted when he introduced the saying of verses 11f. between the question of the disciples (verse 10) and the allegorical interpretation of the parable of the sower (verses 14ff.).[2] After 4 : 11f. verse 13 then gives expression to the Markan view that Jesus struggled to lead the disciples to understanding on the basis of the givenness of the secret of

---

[1] So Wilkens: "The obduracy of the crowd—in contrast with Mark—is not the purpose, but the reason for their inability to understand." (*op. cit.*, p. 312). Bornkamm all but eliminated the distinction by insisting, on the one hand, that the difference between the *hina* and the *hoti* is of little significance here since both Mark and Matthew see in the activity of Jesus the fulfilment of a divine necessity laid down in Scripture, and, on the other hand, that although he recognizes in the saying the fulfilment of a purpose, he suggests that the fulfilment presupposes an already existing condition among the crowds which makes them ripe for it. (*mystērion*, p. 824).

[2] So Marxsen, *op. cit.*, pp. 260f.

the Kingdom (verse 11).[1] The reprimanding of the disciples presupposes that a person with some understanding ought to have been able to grasp the (allegorical) intention of the parable.

The saying may have served a purely stylistic purpose, having been intended to sharpen the attention of the hearers,[2] but it is noteworthy that Matthew left it out even though the understanding that a person with some insight ought to be able to find the "solution" of the parables for himself most closely approximates his own understanding of the parables (cf. Mt. 13 : 12). He apparently left out the saying because he too understood it as a reprimand, but thought that such a reprimand of the disciples would tend to identify them with the stubbornness of the crowds. Nevertheless, Matthew does include the allegorical interpretation (or solution) of the parable of the sower. From his point of view, the interpretation could have been understood as something that was given to those who already had a willingness to understand (Mt. 13 : 12),[3] but more probably he understood it as a mere confirmation of what the disciples had already recognized. Thus, he formulates in verse 18: "You thus, *heard* (i.e., understood) the parable of the sower."

Because Mark accepted the allegorical interpretations of the parables as the fulfillment of their intention, he had to face up to the fact that, according to verses 11f., they were actually told to the outsiders in order to conceal the secret of the Kingdom from them. He tried to reconcile these conceptions of the parables with the statements of verse 34,[4] i.e., by saying that Jesus told parables

---

[1] Cf. Wilkens, *op. cit.*, p. 311.

[2] So Philipp Vielhauer in his Winter 1968/69 seminar on the parables.

[3] So Gerhard Barth: "Whereas the disciples remain completely ignorant ('*gänzlich unverständig*') until the resurrection of Christ in Mark (Mk. 4 : 13; 6 : 51f.; 8 : 17–21; 9 : 6, 10, 32; 10 : 32, cf. Wrede, pp. 101ff.), understanding has already been given to them in Matthew. True, it is not perfect, it is not complete. They are also ignorant time and again, and so a question about the interpretation of a parable or obscure saying can be placed in their mouths in Mt. 13 : 36 and 15 : 15, but Jesus then gives them the understanding, which is explicitly stated." ("Das Gesetzesverständnis des Evangelisten Matthäus," in G. Bornkamm, G. Barth, H. J. Held, *Überlieferung und Auslegung im Mätthaus-Evangelium*, Neukirchen: Neukirchener Verlag, 1961, p. 102; Eng. tr. by Percy Scott, "Matthew's understanding of the Law," in *Tradition and Interpretation in Matthew*, Philadelphia: Westminster Press, 1963, p. 109; cf. Wilkens, *op. cit.*, p. 311).

[4] For this understanding I am indebted to Vielhauer (cf. footnote 2, above). Previously I had thought that verse 34a belonged with the saying of verse 33, which led to a different interpretation also of verse 34b.

(obscure sayings) to them, namely, the crowds (verse 34a), but adding that in privacy he solved them for the disciples (verse 34b). All that Mark really did, however, was to place the two contradictory conceptions side by side without allowing their contradictory intentions to become apparent, i.e., by ignoring the contrast between what happens to "those outside" (verse 11b), and "to you" (verse 11a). He did not resolve the contradictory understandings of the intention of the parables, but, by ignoring the contrast expressed in verse 11, he interpreted these contradictory understandings in the sense of a double purpose of the parables. Furthermore, it apparently slipped his attention that verse 34a as he intended it, namely, that only parables (obscure sayings) were told to the crowds (in order to conceal the secret of the Kingdom from them), now contradicted verse 33b, according to which Jesus spoke in parables as a concession to the ability of his hearers to comprehend, as will be shown below.

Matthew eliminated the second part of Mark's formulation (Mk. 4 : 34b; cf. Mt. 13 : 34f.), probably because in his view a special solution would have been needed for the hard-hearted crowds, not for the disciples.[1]

3. *Jesus told parables as a concession to the limited ability of understanding of his hearers.* (Mk. 4 : 33, cf. verse 33b: "... as they were capable of hearing," i.e., understanding)

If there is something the historian ought to appreciate about Mark, it is the fact that he was not the skillful editor Matthew proved himself to have been—and for this Matthew also deserves our admiration. It was Mark's lack of editorial proficiency which allowed him, in simply honesty to his tradition, to include in his gospel a third conception of the parables which contradicted, and was contradicted by, the other two conceptions mentioned above, which also contradicted each other. According to the saying of Mk. 4 : 33, Jesus told only parables, because of their effectiveness as a means of communicating with an audience. The basic characteristic of a parable suggested by this saying was that its meaning was immediately evident, even to the ordinary hearer. Matthew once more altered his source (Mark) by eliminating the reference to the hearer's ability of comprehension (cf. Mt. 13 : 34), probably because it was

---

[1] So Barth, *op. cit.*, p. 102; Eng. tr., p. 109.

apparent to him from the (allegorical) interpretations that were given to the parables that they could not have been concessions to the people's ability of understanding.

Mk. 4 : 33 may have been the conclusion of a collection of parables which included the parable of the sower (Mk. 4 : 3–9), the growing seed (verses 26–29), and the mustard seed (verses 30–32), from where Mark took them over for his parable chapter. If this was the case, the collection probably did not include the interpretation of the parable of the sower (verses 14–20) from the beginning, since such an interpretation contradicts the correct understanding of the parables expressed in verse 33. In that case it must have been added to the collection at a later stage, but before Mark made use of it, since he apparently encountered the parable with the allegorical interpretation already added to it.[1]

Mark probably thought that with verse 34 he also reconciled the tradition of verse 33 with the others, namely, that the parables were for those who were outside, and that Jesus gave (allegorical) interpetations to them.[2] He probably believed that with his addition of the statements of verse 34, verses 33f. were in agreement, not only with verses 13ff., but also with verses 11f. That Matthew was not satisfied that this was the case is indicated, not only by his elimination of Mk. 4 : 33b and 34b, but also by his other alterations of these verses in Mt. 13 : 34f. Only in Matthew have the contradictions of the Markan account been removed—and admirably.

Conclusion

The conception of the parables to which Mk. 4 : 33 gives expression is undoubtedly the most primitive of the three mentioned above. It reflects a stage in the understanding of the parables before they had become incomprehensible (4 : 11f.) unless they were given a special (allegorical) interpretation (4 : 13ff. and 34). The latter two

---

[1] Cf. above, pp. 12f, 14.

[2] Contrary to Marxsen, *op. cit.*, p. 262, who believes that verse 34a, and only it, is a product of Mark. According to Marxsen, Mark intended to say that Jesus spoke to the crowds only in parables, i.e., in obscure sayings in order to keep the mystery of the Kingdom of God, i.e., his own Messiahship, secret until the time, not even of the resurrection, but of the parousia of Christ. (*op. cit.*, pp. 270f.). The secrecy motif is not an attempt to give a theory of how the parables were intended by Jesus, nor is it an attempt to solve some historical problem. It is rather an expression of how the parables were understood in Mark's own situation. (Cf. *op. cit.*, p. 271., also 263, 267, cf. above, p. 11 footnote 5).

conceptions do not necessarily stand in a chronological or any other direct relationship to each other although the conception which came to expression in verses 11f. is more primitive. Mk. 4 : 33 probably still reflects the original purpose with which Jesus made use of parables, as has been convincingly shown by Adolf Jülicher.[1]

B. The Person of Jesus not Determinative for the Meaning of his Parables

Thus, contrary to the view expressed in Mt. 13 : 12 (cf. Mk. 4 : 25), according to which a certain predisposition was required of Jesus' hearers as a presupposition for understanding his parables, Mk. 4 : 33 has it that Jesus spoke in parables in order to meet the very lack of such a predisposition. It is possible, however, to distinguish between the *pictorial side* ("die Bildhälfte") of a parable which serves to facilitate access to that which is communicated, and the *material side* ("die Sachhälfte"), namely, that which is actually communicated, and to argue that the absence of a predisposition for getting the point of the former does not have to mean an absence of a certain predisposition in the case of the latter. Thus, an understanding of what is communicated in a parable (material side) may require a certain predisposition, e.g., acceptance of the fact that the ministry of Jesus was the manifestation of the breaking in of the Kingdom of God, which nevertheless leaves unaffected the absence of any particular predisposition for understanding the pictorial side which serves to clarify what is communicated. In this case an understanding of the material side presupposes a certain predisposition towards the person who tells the parable. This conception of the parables is widely advocated. So, for example, by Jeremias.

After expressing his admiration for the convincing way in which Jülicher disposed of the allegorical interpretation of the parables as

---

[1] *Op. cit.*, pp. 44–118; cf. 119–121. Cf. also Marxsen, *op. cit.*, pp. 263 and 265; Jeremias, *op. cit.*, pp. (12), 14f.; Eng. tr., pp. 18f.; C. H. Dodd, *The Parables of the Kingdom*, New York: Charles Scribner's Sons, 1961, also as a Fontana paperback, Glasgow: William Collins Sons and Co. Ltd., 1961, pp. 13–21. (References below will be to the latter).

However, although Jülicher recognized that Mk. 4 : 33 appears to lend support to the understanding of the parables as ways of speaking intended to promote understanding, he thinks that this is contradicted by verse 34; not by 34a, but by 34b. (*op. cit.*, pp. 119f.). As has been indicated above, verse 34b does contradict verse 33b, but then verse 33 should be interpreted on its own, not with verse 34b.

a false procedure, he contends that Jülicher did only half of what was needed. According to Jeremias, Jülicher was misled by his concern to free the interpretation of the arbitrariness of the allegorical method. "The best safeguard against such arbitrariness, according to him, existed in taking the parables as a piece of real life, and in each case to draw from them only one thought, the one with the broadest possible meaning."[1] In the latter, according to Jeremias, lay Jülicher's error. The result was that, according to Jülicher's interpretation, Jesus proclaimed the truly religious humanity in the parables. "Nothing remained of their eschatological import. Imperceptably Jesus became 'the apostle of progress' (II, p. 483); a teacher of wisdom, who impressed (on the minds of his hearers) ethical maxims and a simplified theology in telling images and stories."[2] According to Jeremias, a break-through in the main work on the parables, namely, the task of regaining their original meaning, was made by Dodd, who for the first time really succeeded in the attempt to place the parables back in the situation of the life of Jesus.[3]

Dodd himself gave the following summary of his understanding of the parables. "They use all the resources of dramatic illustration to help men to see that in the events before their eyes—in the miracles of Jesus, His appeal to men and its results, the blessedness that comes to those who follow Him, and the hardening of those who reject Him; in the tragic conflict of the Cross, and the tribulation of the disciples; in the fateful choice before the Jewish people, and the disasters that threaten—God is confronting them in His kingdom, power and glory. This world has become the scene of a divine drama, in which the eternal issues are laid bare. It is the hour of decision. It is realized eschatology."[4]

Jeremias criticized Dodd on two points, the one being that "the onesidedness of his concept of the Kingdom ... resulted in a shortening of the eschatology (i.e., in the sense of Dodd's 'realized eschatology'), which did not remain without influence on the otherwise masterly exegesis."[5] Dodd subsequently accepted, as a possible alternative for the "not altogether felicitous term 'realized eschato-

---

[1] *Op. cit.*, pp. (13), 15; Eng. tr., p. 19.
[2] *Ad loc.*
[3] *Op. cit.*, pp. (13–15), 16f.; Eng. tr., pp. 20f.
[4] *Op. cit.*, pp. 147f.
[5] *Op. cit.*, pp. (15), 17; Eng. tr., p. 21.

logy',," Ernst Haenchen's suggestion[1] of "'sich realisierende Eschatologie,' which I like, but cannot translate into English."[2] In his
translation of Jeremias' *Parables of Jesus*, S. H. Hooke translated
the phrase "an eschatology that is in process of realization,"[3] which
at least renders the meaning adequately.

Jeremias furthermore criticized Dodd for limiting himself to the
parables of the Kingdom. He himself accordingly expanded his
inquiry to all the parables of Jesus, in an attempt to recapture their
original meaning and so to recapture the *"ipsissima vox* of Jesus."[4]
At the end of his inquiry he concluded: "... all the parables of Jesus
compel the hearers to take a position in relation to his person and
his mission. For they are all filled with the 'secret of the sovereignty
of God' (Mk. 4 : 11)—i.e., the certainty of the eschatology in process
of realization. The moment of fulfilment is there. That is their
fundamental tone."[5]

From the point of view of the understanding of the parables
suggested in this paper, the interpretation of Dodd and Jeremias can
only be regarded as a regression to a more refined form of allegorical
interpretation. Dodd and Jeremias reintroduced precisely that
which the primitive Christian community had originally introduced
with the allegorical interpretations, i.e., the involvement of a
Christology in the parables. Jeremias could indeed find support for
this from Ernst Fuchs, who "strongly emphasizes that the parables
are implicit Christological self-attestations."[6] He meant in particular
Fuchs' article "Bemerkungen zur Gleichnisauslegung,"[7] in which
he indicated that he does not see why Jesus could not have *concealed*
himself in his parables. "... why should it not be possible for the
historical Jesus to be the concealed Christ?"[8]

---

[1] Mediated by Jeremias, cf. Jeremias, *op. cit.*, pp. (194), 227; Eng. tr., p.
230.
[2] *The Interpretation of the Fourth Gospel*, Cambridge: University Press,
1960, p. 447, footnote 1.
[3] *Op. cit.*, p. 230.
[4] *Op. cit.*, pp. (16), 18; Eng. tr., p. 22.
[5] *Op. cit.*, pp. (194), 227; Eng. tr., p. 230.
[6] Jeremias, *op. cit.*, pp. (194), 227; Eng. tr., p. 230.
[7] *Theologische Literaturzeitung*, 79 (1954), cols. 345–348, now in *Zur Frage
nach dem historischen Jesus, Gesammelte Aufsätze* II, Tübingen: J. C. B. Mohr
(Paul Siebeck), 1960, pp. 136–142. (References below will be to Fuchs'
collected essays, also to the Eng. tr. by Andrew Scobie, *Studies of the Historical
Jesus*, London: S. C. M. Press Ltd., 1964, for those articles that have been
translated).
[8] *Op. cit.*, II, p. 141.

Fuchs substantiated this by arguing that the parable of the workers in the vineyard (Mt. 20 : 1–16) only becomes really meaningful when it is understood to refer to Jesus. "Because in Jesus God made manifest, not only that in all sternness he was a gracious God, but, in addition, that he wanted to be *understood* historically *as* such a God by those who do *not* see his goodness active in the world."[1] Another example of such an involvement of Jesus in his own proclamation, according to Fuchs, is the parable of the prodigal son (Lk. 15 : 11–32). He states, contrary to what he refers to as the tendency to relate the father in the parable too immediately to God, that in the action of the father Jesus defended his own conduct. Fuchs understands, of course, that Jesus grounded his conduct in the will of God. "Jesus risks it to enforce the will of God in such a way that he himself appears in the place of God."[2] As is well known, Fuchs understands this to be true not only for the teaching of Jesus, but also for his conduct as a whole. According to him it can be clearly said of Jesus "that he could very well under the symbol of the *basileia* point to a definite act of the graciousness of God, because he celebrated, and not only once, with publicans and sinners, indeed not the messianic meal, but a meal celebrating the *basileia* of God."[3]

Fuchs is aware that "Jülicher, and indeed not only he, would consider this understanding (of the parables) as already allegorical interpretation ..."[4] This, of course, does not deter him. To the question whether Mark did not already understand the historical Jesus as the concealed Christ, he retorts: "And has it been established so conclusively that Mark was wrong historically?"[5]

A more consistent non-allegorical interpretation would be that a predisposition was required neither for the understanding of the pictorial side of the parables, nor for that of their material side. In this case the only claim Jesus would have made on his hearers, irrespective of whether they were his followers or his opponents, would have been that they had to recognize that he interpreted the situation correctly. Only when the original intentions of the parables were lost, were they conceived of as being incomprehensible to those outside the realm of believers who did not recognize the Christolo-

---

[1] *Op. cit.*, II, p. 140.
[2] *Op. cit.*, II, p. 154; Eng. tr., p. 20.
[3] *Op. cit.*, II, p. 223; Eng. tr., p. 35.
[4] *Op. cit.*, II, p. 138.
[5] *Op. cit.*, II, p. 141.

gical significance of Jesus. Only then were they understood to have been used as a device to confuse outsiders (Mk. 4 : 11f.), or to have required (allegorical) interpretations for the insiders (Mk. 4 : 13ff., 34, cf. Mt. 13 : 12). Thus, for example, originally the parable of the banquet (Mt. 22 : 1–10; Lk. 14 : 16–24) appears to have been directed more specifically to the pious opponents of Jesus in order to make evident to them why it was the outcasts and not they who participated in the Kingdom of God.[1] Faith was not required for an understanding of this parable. This is also true in the case of the parables of the lost sheep (Mt. 18 : 12–14; Lk. 15 : 1–7), the lost coin (Lk. 15 : 8–10) and probably the prodigal son (Lk. 15 : 11–32).

Jeremias has shown that there was a strong tendency in the handing down of the parable tradition to alter the parables which Jesus spoke to the crowds and his opponents into parables intended for his disciples.[2] This is found in all three of the synoptic gospels, and Jeremias gives a long list of cases where it took place.[3] This is all part of the tendency of the tradition to narrow down the meaning of parables. Thus, it comes somewhat as a surprise that Jeremias could conclude that "all the parables of Jesus compel the hearers to take in a position relation to his person and his mission."[4]

C. The Grounding of the Meaning of the Parables of Jesus in the Situation of his Hearers

Contrary to the above-mentioned interpretations it is suggested here that the parables of Jesus were not intended to disclose the nature of his mission and that their validity did not depend on his authority to "enforce the will of God" (Fuchs), but on their effectiveness in interpreting or disclosing the truth about man's situation in his world. Thus, for example, the truth which is disclosed by the parable of the compassionate Samaritan (Lk. 10 : 20–37) would remain unaffected even if it were determined that it was in

---

[1] Cf. however, Eta Linnemann (*Gleichnisse Jesu*, Göttingen: Vandenhoeck und Ruprecht, 1961, 4th ed., 1966, pp. 94–103; Eng. tr. by John Sturdy, *Parables of Jesus*, London: SPCK., pp. 88–97), who interprets it as a crisis parable. But in that case it was directed indiscriminately to a general audience and not specifically to his followers, not even to mention "believers."

[2] *Op. cit.*, pp. (31, cf. 23–31), 38, cf. 29–39; Eng. tr., pp. 41f., cf. 33–42.

[3] *Ibid.*, pp. (31), 38; Eng. tr., p. 42.

[4] *Ibid.*, pp. (194), 227; Eng. tr., p. 230.

fact never told by Jesus. A most convincing case is made by Luise Schottroff[1] that along with the other specifically Lukan parables, it is a product of Luke himself answering the question of the legal expert trying to justify himself in verse 29: "who is my neighbor?" The question is answered by telling a parable which clarifies the situation. This is the true function of a parable.

This means that there is a certain priority of the situation of Jesus and his hearers, which he disclosed by articulating it in his parables. His words did not create their world. Rather it was their world which called forth his words as its disclosure. In terms of the New Hermeneutic, the world of his hearers, which was also his world, was the reality which found articulation in his ministry. In his parables he suggested their world to his hearers, and relied upon them to recognize that he interpreted it correctly. In his association with publicans and sinners he did not *bring* the love and forgiveness of God, but *affirmed* its presence among them by articulating it. This does not mean that the world, made conscious through its articulation in the parables, was not, in a sense, re-created. By articulating the world in which he and his hearers found themselves, the words of Jesus were at the same time liberating and judging, so that a person may very well have responded to his teaching in the awareness that everything had become new.

Jesus apparently found it proper to affirm the world in which he and his contemporaries found themselves. He did not strive for another world such as the Pharisees hoped to attain through legal piety. His conduct also gave witness to the fact that he no longer considered the ascetic piety of John the Baptist appropriate. It was with the religious, moral and social outcasts of Jewish society that he associated. They were the ones who were forced by their circumstances to accept as theirs the world in which they were living. Unlike the Pharisees, the Baptist and his disciples, and other pious groups, they had no hope of participating in some other world which would have freed them from the necessity of accepting the reality of their present world. And yet, Jesus was confident, they were the ones who experienced the joy of the Kingdom of God. He presented them in the parable of the great banquet (Mt. 22 : 1–10; Lk. 14 :16–24) as the originally uninvited guests who accepted the invitation

---

[1] In a personal conversation in which she indicated this as the research in which she was engaged, in anticipation of a future publication.

after those for whom the banquet had been intended refused to come.

But then it would be incorrect to say that Jesus *introduced* the Kingdom of God with his ministry.[1] Rather, he *announced* that it had already arrived; that it was already present in the world in which they lived, and he identified himself with those who were prepared to receive it, because they had no means of escaping the reality of the world in which they were living.

To the question how it had been possible for Jesus to recognize and thus proclaim that the expected Kingdom of God had in fact in a sense been present among the *am ha'ares*, the early Church responded by assuming that he had had divine authority. Today we can recognize this as a mere cypher, expressing the conviction that Jesus in fact did interpret his world and that of his hearers correctly, in a similar way to the encyphering of the effectiveness with which Augustus Caesar brought peace to a world that had been torn by more than two centuries of strife, in the legend that he was the divinely generated son of Apollo. It is not necessary to deny that Jesus' call to decision (e.g., Mt. 11 : 6, "... blessed is he who does not take offense in me") implied a Christology (Bultmann),[2] or even

---

[1] So, e.g., even Rudolf Bultmann, *Theologie des Neuen Testaments*, Tübingen: J. C. B. Mohr (Paul Siebeck), 3rd ed. 1958, pp. 3–10; Eng. tr. by K. Grobel, *The Theology of the New Testament*, New York: Charles Scribner's Sons, vol. 1, 1951, vol. 2, 1955, pp. 4–11. So, e.g., explicitly on p. 8 (Eng. tr., p. 9): "Fundamentally, thus, *he himself in his person is the 'sign of the time'*," i.e., that the Kingdom of God was breaking in.

[2] Cf. Bultmann's statement that "Jesus' call to decision implies a Christology." (*Theologie des Neuen Testaments*, p. 46, cf. pp. 8f.; Eng. tr., p. 43, cf. p. 9f. Also *Glauben und Verstehen. Gesammelte Aufsätze*, Tübingen: J. C. B. Mohr (Paul Siebeck), vol. I, pp. 204 and 266). As is well known, Hans Conzelmann made use of this statement of Bultmann in his interpretation of the relation between the proclamation of the primitive Church and the ministry of Jesus. So in the following statement: "Although the situation has become a new one, the continuity between the Church and the historical Jesus is preserved. This is achieved (by the fact that Jesus already involved his person in the future salvation, (by the fact) that his call to a decision implied a Christology (Bultmann, NT. 44)." ("Eschatologie IV. Im Urchristentum," *Die Religion in Geschichte und Gegenwart*, 3rd ed. edited by Kurt Galling, Tübingen: J. C. B. Mohr (Paul Siebeck), 1957ff. (abbreviated *RGG*.[3] below), II, col. 668. Conzelmann's reference to p. 44 of Bultmann's *Theologie des Neuen Testaments* is to the 2nd edition, which is the same as p. 46 of the 3rd ed. referred to above). Cf. also "Jesus Christus," *RGG*.[3], III, cols. 631–633; furthermore James M. Robinson, *The New Quest of the Historical Jesus*, London: S. C. M. Press, 1959, pp. 18f., and 111, footnote 3, and *Kerygma und historischer Jesus*, Zürich/Stuttgart: Zwingli Verlag, 1960, p. 24, footnote 6, and p. 138, 2nd ed. 1967, p. 41, footnote 77, and p. 201.

better, that his *conduct* implied a Christology (Fuchs),[1] if Christology can be understood as nothing other than a cypher for the hermeneutic of reality, i.e., of the world in which he found himself, with which Jesus challenged his hearers, irrespective of their disposition towards him. This is a question of great significance with which we will have to concern ourselves below.

---

[1] *Op. cit.*, p. 185, footnote 36, cf. also p. 403; Eng. tr., p. 189.

CHAPTER TWO

JESUS AND THE KINGDOM OF GOD

A. The Future and the Presence of the Kingdom in the Synoptic Tradition

One can go yet a step further in the understanding of the ministry of Jesus. If it was characteristic of his ministry that he turned away from the world-denying piety of John the Baptist (cf. Mt. 11 : 18f., Lk. 7 : 33f.) when he recognized that in a sense the Kingdom of God was already experienced by the *am ha'ares*, the people of the land, then the parables which emphasize the crisis in the face of the breaking in of the Kingdom of God should be considered as probably belonging to the earlier Baptist phase of his ministry, if indeed these parables are to be considered authentic at all. The parables in question include The Door-keeper (Mk. 13 : 33–37), The Guest without a Wedding Garment (Mt. 22 : 11–13) and The Ten Maidens (Mt. 25 : 1–13).[1] All tradition which emphasizes the *coming* of the Kingdom of God should be regarded as unresolved remnants of the earlier influence of the Baptist—if it did not in fact originate *at an earlier stage* in the ministry of Jesus when he was still closer to the Baptist, or even from the Baptist himself. The authenticity of all sayings which explicitly express the expectation of the Kingdom of God in the near future, is questioned by Eta Linnemann.[2]

That the eschatological urgency is not a distinctive feature of these parables compared with the Jewish environment out of which Jesus came is evident when one considers the Qumran literature.

---

[1] The original point of the latter parable was probably that the five "foolish" maidens "slumbered and fell asleep" (cf. verse 5), and so missed entering with the bridegroom when he arrived (verses 10–12). An interpretation such as this is called for by the concluding "Be on the alert (*grēgoreite*), therefore, because you do not know the day or the hour" (verse 13), which ties in with the now somewhat superfluous reference to the fact that the maidens—in the present form, all of them—slumbered and fell asleep (verse 5). Matthew, of course, understood the parable as an allegory condemning those who had not prepared for an extended period of waiting for the parousia, and thus had given up the expectation.

[2] *Op. cit.* (cf. above, p. 22, footnote 1), pp. 138–141; Eng. tr., pp. 132–136.

Like the Baptist and Jesus, the Qumran sect understood itself to have lived in the end time.[1] What distinguishes the understanding of these parables from the eschatological urgency as it was experienced in Qumran, is the fact that the urgency was carefully guarded from outsiders by the sect,[2] whereas Jesus proclaimed it openly,[3] as the Baptist had already done before him.[4] This guarding of the secret about the end time in Qumran has a remarkable parallel in the saying in Mark that the secret of the Kingdom of God was concealed from those outside (Mk. 4 : 11f., cf. par.s).[5] This saying, however, was apparently not formulated in dependence on Qumran, but as a solution to the problem of the incomprehensibility of the parables in some primitive Christian circles.[6] Nevertheless, the idea of keeping what is known about the end secret from outsiders is clearly parallel in Qumran and in this saying.[7]

Thus it appears that the Qumran sect, like John the Baptist, shared the eschatological urgency of the crisis parables, but not the openness with which this was proclaimed. The latter was shared with the parables by the Baptist, in contrast, not only with the Qumran sect, but also with the subsequent primitive Christian understanding as expressed in the saying of Mk. 4 : 11f.

---

[1] The nature of the Qumran literature does not make it possible to substantiate this particular point by simple reference to relevant sections in this literature without appropriate commentary. Such commentary, however, would require too great a diversion here. For an extensive review of the research on the relation between Qumran and the New Testament cf. Herbert Braun, "Qumran und das Neue Testament. Ein Bericht über 10 Jahre Forschung (1950–1959)," *Theologische Rundschau* 28–30 (1962–1964), which has now appeared in book form as vol. I of *Qumran und das Neue Testament*, Tübingen: J. C. B. Mohr (Paul Siebeck), 1966, 2 vols. Specifically relevant for our present concern is the section "Eschatologie," vol. II, pp. 265-286, and there in particular pp. 266, 273, 274, 281f., and 286. For Braun's own discussion with relevant references, cf. *Spätjüdisch-häretischer und frühchristlicher Radikalismus*, Tübingen: J. C. B. Mohr (Paul Siebeck), 1957 (2 vols.), vol. I, pp. 32f., 51–53, 109–111; vol. II, p. 46, footnote 1 (which continues into p. 53).

[2] Cf. Braun, *Radikalismus*, vol. I, pp. 17f., 50–53, cf. vol. II, pp. 18–23, 46, footnote 1, paragraph 6 (on pp. 50–52); also *Qumran und das Neue Testament*, vol. II, p. 266.

[3] Cf. Braun, *Radikalismus*, vol. II, pp. 18–23; *Qumran und das Neue Testament*, vol. II, p. 276.

[4] Cf. Braun, *Qumran und das Neue Testament*, vol. II, p. 273.

[5] Cf. Braun, *Radikalismus*, vol. II, p. 21, footnote 4.

[6] Cf. above, part I, section I, A, 1. Cf. also Braun, *ad loc.*, who emphasizes the differences in the choice of words, the absence of a dualism in the gospel saying, and the absence of Is. 6 : 9f. in this context in the Qumran literature.

[7] So also Braun, *ad loc.*

The situation of the crisis parables appears to have been essentially still that of John the Baptist as expressed in sayings such as "Convert yourselves, for the Kingdom of the Heavens is at hand" (Mt. 3 : 2, cf. 4 : 17, according to which Jesus commenced his own proclamation with the identical words): "You brood of serpents! Who showed you to flee from the coming wrath?" (Mt. 3:7; Lk. 3 : 7) and "... the axe is already at the root of the trees. Every tree, therefore, which does not bear good fruit will be cut down and thrown into fire" (Mt. 3 : 10; Lk. 3 : 9).

Attributing the crisis parables to Jesus is questioned here not on the basis of new criteria for distinguishing tradition which reflects the contribution of Jesus, but as a result of a more stringent application than is usually the case of the existing criterion. This criterion was formulated by Ernst Käsemann as follows: "We have relatively firm ground under our feet in a single instance only, namely, when tradition, due to whatever the circumstances may be, can be derived, neither from Judaism nor from primitive Christianity, and especially when Jewish Christianity toned down or altered the tradition which came down to it (because it considered this tradition) as too sharp."[1] It should be noted that only what is *distinctive* of Jesus can be determined in this way. There is no way of determining the authenticity or not of tradition which conforms with the Jewish environment out of which Jesus came.

In his recent book on the teaching of Jesus, Norman Perrin refers to this as the *criterion of dissimilarity*.[2] A decided methodological weakness of this book, however, is the fact that Perrin introduces a second criterion, the *criterion of coherence*.[3] The largest portion of the material which he accepted as authentic was introduced on the basis of the latter criterion, which in fact contradicts the former. Material which would have to be excluded by the first criterion

---

[1] "Das Problem des historischen Jesus," *Zeitschrift für Theologie und Kirche*, 51 (1954), p. 144, now in *Exegetische Versuche und Besinnungen*, Göttingen: Vandenhoeck und Ruprecht, vol. I, 1960, p. 205; Eng. tr. by W. J. Montague, "The Problem of the Historical Jesus," *Essays on New Testament Themes*, London: SCM Press, 1964, p. 37; cf. Bultmann, *Geschichte der synoptischen Tradition*, Göttingen: Vandenhoeck und Ruprecht, 4th ed. with an *Ergänzungsheft*, 1957, p. 222; Eng. tr. by John Marsh, *History of the Synoptic Tradition*, Oxford: Basil Blackwell, New York: Harper and Row, 1963, p. 205.
[2] Norman Perrin, *Rediscovering the Teaching of Jesus*, New York and Evanston: Harper and Row, 1967, p. 39.
[3] *Op. cit.*, p. 43.

because it is not dissimilar, is admitted by the second one because it shows coherence with material already accepted on the basis of the former. This procedure does not serve historical discrimination, but the desire to have as full a picture of the teaching of Jesus as possible.

The reconstruction of such a picture in any case appears impossible. The criterion of "dissimilarity" may serve as an indication of how Jesus distinguished himself from his background—although there is no reason to assume that everything that is distinctive in the synoptic gospels could only have come from him—but there is no certain way of determining what part of that background he preserved. The criterion of coherence is completely arbitrary. It would depend on the interpreter to determine what part of the non-distinctive synoptic gospel material he considers coherent with that which is distinctive, and what part not.

This second criterion of Perrin could, of course, as in fact it does, serve to include the futuristic eschatological tradition as part of the teaching of Jesus. Nevertheless, the responsibility rests on him to show why this tradition should not be regarded as remnants of the influence of the Baptist, or of the general apocalyptic thinking of the time on Jesus. As has already been suggested, some of this material may in fact have been products of the Baptist that have been preserved and confused with the tradition of Jesus. Perrin explicitly accepts that *"the nature of the synoptic tradition is such that the burden of proof will be upon the claim to authenticity."*[1] Surely this cannot apply only to the elimination of material which originated from the primitive church.

Käsemann suggested a further significant factor for the understanding of historical developments, such as we are considering, when he stated that he could "conceive of historical sequences ('Geschichtsverlaufe') only in the tension between continuity and discontinuity." Only in this way is he "able to speak of history, the process of which is constituted by changes in direction, setbacks, upheavals, and new beginnings."[2] Käsemann stated this in connec-

---

[1] *Op. cit.*, p. 39. Perrin's emphasis.

[2] "Sackgassen im Streit um den historischen Jesus," *Exegetische Versuche und Besinnungen*, vol. II, p. 43; Eng. tr. by W. J. Montague, "Blind Alleys in the 'Jesus of History' controvercy," *New Testament Questions of Today*, London: SCM Press Ltd., 1969, p. 37. Cf., however, the criticism of the terminology "continuity" and "discontinuity" by Gerhard Ebeling, *Theologie und Verkündigung*, Tübingen: J. C. B. Mohr (Paul Siebeck), 1963, pp. 57f., as well as Käsemann's reply, *ad loc.*

tion with the problem of the relation between the historical Jesus and the early Christian proclamation, but clearly intended it as a statement that would apply to history in general.

In accordance with such an understanding, it would not be the continuation by Jesus of what he received from his environment that would be most significant,but the way in which he moved beyond that which he received, i.e., the tension brought about by the discontinuity with his environment. Thus we would go only half way in our understanding of Jesus if we do not distinguish his own contribution from that which he inherited and preserved from his environment, particularly since the inclusion of material from the latter in the synoptic tradition was probably determined less by what Jesus intended than by the apparently limited discrimination with which the tradition was collected and handed down.

Ultimately the question how far Jesus himself actually developed this discontinuity is of secondary importance. He may have been prevented by his death on the cross from following through consistently all the way in the new direction in which he had started to move. What is of primary importance is the direction of this movement. Thus, it would be unfair to the historical Jesus, and also unwarranted, not to consider the possibility that it was inherent in his contribution to recognize a far greater discontinuity with his environment than the synoptic tradition seems to indicate. A strong indication that this may have been the case can be found in the fact that no attempt to solve the so-called problem of the eschatological tension between the future and the presence of the Kingdom of God in the teaching of Jesus has been completely successful.[1] This may be due to the fact that it is not an inherent problem in the proclamation of Jesus, but a product of the tension between the continuity and discontinuity in historical sequences about which Käsemann speaks. It becomes insoluble only when it is not recognized that the futuristic eschatology in the synoptic gospels originated in continuity with the Jewish apocalyptic environment out of which Jesus came, with which he found himself not only in a growing tension, but, as far as the futuristic eschatology is concerned, in outright discontinuity. The Jewish apocalyptic environment was again typical of the primitive church as a whole, which explains why the church

---

[1] For a discussion of this problem, cf. Norman Perrin, *The Kingdom of God in the Teaching of Jesus*, London: SCM Press, and Philadelphia: Westminster Press, 1963.

found no difficulty in handing down the futuristic eschatology tradition on the assumption that it represented the intention of Jesus. Thus, solutions of the problem of the tension between the future and the presence of the Kingdom of God in the synoptic tradition based on the assumption that it was an inherent tension in the teaching of Jesus may have to be considered at best as good solutions to a mistaken problem.

This does not exclude inherent tensions in the teaching of Jesus. Such tensions did indeed exist, for example, in the fact that he recognized those who were apparently most remotely removed from the Kingdom of God, the people of the land; the poor, the hungry and those that mourn (Lk. 6 : 20b–21; cf. Mt. 5 : 3, 6, 4), as the ones to whom the Kingdom belonged. This tension was maintained by the fact that the Kingdom was not identified with their poverty, hunger and mourning. Unlike John the Baptist, Jesus was not an ascetic, but someone who apparently intended to enjoy life. (Cf. Mt. 11 : 18f; Lk. 7 : 33f).

Thus, if the phrase "authentic tradition" can still mean anything, it would have to be that it refers to tradition which gives authentic expression to the discontinuity of which the teaching of Jesus became representative. The actual teaching of Jesus remains largely unknown to us, because ill-defined. Except for individual cases where it may be possible to determine with a high degree of probability that material does contain historical data about Jesus,[1] the only relatively firm ground we have is the discontinuity itself. But this discontinuity cannot serve as a reliable means of rediscovering the teaching of Jesus; for two reasons. First, as Perrin's principle of coherence presupposes, because the *discontinuity does not represent all of the teaching of Jesus*. This remains true even though this second principle does not solve the problem. And secondly, because *the discontinuity itself is not a certain indication that material did originate from Jesus*. The mere fact that material is marked by discontinuity does not mean that it could only have come from Jesus. This is where the criterion of coherence, however, could serve further historical discrimination, but only if it is used, not as an *alternate* criterion, which is what Perrin did with it, but as a *second* test which material has to pass, not in order to establish, but only to strengthen its claim to authenticity. Material, thus, which passes the test of

---

[1] So, e.g., the tradition of Mt. 11 : 2–19. Cf. below, pp. 45–54.

dissimilarity would only come into serious consideration as authentic if it also passes the test of coherence, i.e., when it is coherent with what may have been determined otherwise, on purely historical grounds, to have been true of Jesus. On the whole, however, the teaching of Jesus will remain un-rediscovered.

But then, the significance of tradition does not depend on whether or not it originated from Jesus, but on whether it has something relevant to disclose. So, for example, as has already been stated, it matters little who was responsible for the telling of the parable of the compassionate Samaritan. The question is whether it is a meaningful expression of man's situation in the world. Thus also, the fact that sayings attributed to Jesus are still meaningful today is not due to, or dependent on, the fact that he may have said them, but because they are still capable of giving meaningful expression to man's situation in the world. This means that man's situation in the world as Jesus or whoever else experienced and expressed it, and as we still experience it today, is the true author of these sayings. The same would be true of sayings which give expression to the way in which the world was experienced *in a particular historical situation*, except that then such sayings would not have to be meaningful expressions of how man experiences his world today. However, that does not exclude the possibility that one could learn to understand his own, i.e., present situation in the world better from such sayings.

B. The Problem of the Authority of Jesus

Instead of books on the ministry or teaching of Jesus, what is called for is a book on the discontinuity with which his ministry was associated. A serious weakness in most books on the ministry or teaching of Jesus is the fact that they are based on the assumption that he must in some sense be the final authority, and thus make everything dependent on the impracticable task of rediscovering with at least approximate completeness what he actually taught. Even more serious as a problem for *critical* research is the assumption of such an authority in itself. By its very nature critical inquiry subjects its material to a higher, i.e., critical principle. In such an inquiry Jesus cannot be the final authority since his teaching is itself subject to critical scrutiny. This, nevertheless, is frequently the case. So, for example, in Perrin's *Rediscovering the Teaching of*

Jesus, which is, and is intended to be, a critical inquiry, the authoritative nature of the teaching of Jesus is reaffirmed.

Perrin suggests that "we have the right to appeal to our limited, but real, historical knowledge of Jesus" in order to distinguish "true from false" among the multitude of conflicting and competing kerygmata; where everything from radical right racism to revolutionary Christian humanism is proclaimed as kerygma, and as Christion.[1] So also in his conclusion: "... in face of the varities of Christian proclamation and in view of the claim inherent in the nature of the synoptic gospel material (earthly Jesus = risen Lord), we may and we must use such historical knowledge of Jesus as we possess to test the validity of the claim of any given form of the Church's proclamation to be *Christian* proclamation."[2] Thus it appears that the historical Jesus is in some sense the norm for the Christian faith. "The significance of the historical Jesus for the Christian faith is that knowledge of this Jesus may be used as a means of testing the claims of the Christs presented in the competing kerygmata to be Jesus Christ."[3] If Perrin is serious about this, it would mean that no kerygma can any longer be considered Christian, since none would be capable of passing the test, particularly not if one includes an apocalyptic concept of the Kingdom of God as part of the teaching of Jesus. In this regard one can only admire the consistency of Albert Schweitzer who insisted that the historical Jesus, freed from the bonds of dogma, returned to his own time.[4] Apparently Perrin does not consider it necessary for Jesus to return to his own time, although he is aware of the impact of Schweitzer's "thoroughgoing eschatology" on the liberal presentations of the life of Jesus. "The Jesus of the older liberal faith-image has to be transformed precisely because he was, in some fundamental respects, inconsistent with the historical Jesus revealed to us as a result of the work set in motion by *konsequente Eschatologie*."[5]

---

[1] *Rediscovering the Teaching of Jesus*, p. 244.

[2] *Op. cit.*, pp. 247f.

[3] *Op. cit.*, p. 244.

[4] *Von Reimarus zu Wrede*, Tübingen: J. C. B. Mohr, 1906; since the 2nd ed. *Geschichte der Leben-Jesu-Forschung*, 1913ff., now with an introduction by James M. Robinson as Siebenstern-Taschenbuch 77–80, p. 620; Eng. tr., from the 1st ed. by W. Montgomery, *The Quest of the Historical Jesus*, London: A. and C. Black, 1910, now as a MacMillan paperback, 2nd printing 1962, p. 399.

[5] *Op. cit.*, p. 246.

It can safely be assumed that Perrin does not intend that a
"*Christian* proclamation" should conform to Jesus' understanding
of the end as has been recovered by Schweitzer, and by Johannes
Weiss[1] before him. But the question is how the teaching of Jesus can
at the same time be normative and subject to a norm, because it is
evident that there must be some other norm than the proclamation
of Jesus itself by means of which his eschatological understanding is
revised. It may be objected that we do not have to revise the eschatology of Jesus, but only to reinterpret it. The question is what is
reinterpreted: The eschatology of Jesus? But surely this is what
Weiss and Schweitzer did when they showed that the earlier liberal
interpretations of Jesus' concept of the Kingdom of God were false.
In this case, indeed, the object of reinterpretation was the eschatology of Jesus, and his actual teaching was the controlling factor for
the reinterpretation, which depended entirely on how much of it
could be rediscovered. But with this reinterpretation Jesus was
allowed to return to his own time because it became clear that his
(apocalyptic) eschatology could not be considered normative for the
present. The reinterpretation of the eschatology of Jesus did not
confirm his authority, but revealed that he was bound to his own
time.

Thus, it is clearly not the teaching of Jesus which is normative.
What has to be reinterpreted, if his message is to be meaningful for
today, is not his eschatology, but that which he experienced and
expressed in terms of his eschatology. *The teaching of Jesus was itself
an interpretation*, i.e., of man's situation in his world. A reinterpretation is not of a previous interpretation, but replaces a previous
interpretation, either because it was mistaken—as was the case with
the liberal interpretations of the eschatology of Jesus—or because
the previous interpretation is no longer adequate, e.g., because its
language is no longer an adequate medium for understanding—as is
the case with the teaching of Jesus. Thus, what Jesus experienced
and expressed, i.e., interpreted, in terms of his eschatological
language—which is no longer an adequate medium for understanding—has to be experienced anew *through his interpretation*, and
then expressed, i.e., reinterpreted in a language which is an adequate
medium for today. Strictly speaking, it is not specifically what Jesus

---

[1] *Die Predigt Jesu vom Reiche Gottes*, 1st ed. 1892, 2nd revised ed. 1900,
3rd ed. edited by Ferdinand Hahn, Göttingen: Vandenhoeck und Ruprecht,
1964.

experienced and expressed which is of primary concern for us, but that which was experienced and expressed in the synoptic gospels as a discontinuity with the Jewish environment out of which Jesus came. Jesus has significance for us here only in as far as his ministry was part of this discontinuity.

What Jesus experienced and expressed is not recoverable except in the language in which he experienced and expressed it. Thus, his language must be understood correctly, which makes the reinterpretation of the eschatology of Jesus by Weiss and Schweitzer an indispensable prerequisite for a reinterpretation of what he experienced and expressed in his teaching. Furthermore, what he experienced and expressed in his teaching is not recoverable as a "Ding an sich," free from the language in which it was experienced and expressed. Thus, what is called for is, first, that what Jesus experienced and expressed, i.e., what he understood about man's situation in his world, should be recovered through the apocalyptic eschatological language in which he experienced and expressed this understanding, and then, this should be reinterpreted in a language that is an adequate medium of understanding, i.e., of experiencing and expressing this understanding today.

But then it is not the language or teaching of Jesus which is normative, but the situation of man in the world which found articulation in his language and teaching. This situation in the world, thus, is the real "author" of his language and teaching. His language was meaningful only in as far as it was a valid articulation of man's situation in the world, and it would be meaningful for today only if, and as far as, it validly articulates man's present situation in the world, or at least contributes toward such an articulation. In all cases the norm for the validity of the language and teaching of Jesus derives from that which it articulates. Thus, the real norm for a reinterpretation of the teaching of Jesus for today can only be man's present situation in the world. His teaching would be meaningful only if it contributes toward a better understanding of this situation, by participating in its articulation.

This is what we have learned from Rudolf Bultmann whose program of demythologizing is an attempt to reinterpret in existentialist language what Jesus and the New Testament writers expressed in mythological language. His existentialist reinterpretation was in turn based on the reinterpretation of the language of Jesus and the New Testament writers by historians of religion such as Johannes Weiss[1] and Wilhelm Bousset,[2] to mention only two. Bultmann expressed his understanding most concisely as follows. "The real intention of the myth is not to give an objective world view; rather, in it comes to expression how man understands himself in his world."[3] Unfortunately Bultmann then immediately proceeds to narrow down the intention of the mythological language when he states: "... the myth does not want to be interpreted cosmologically, but anthropologically—better still: existentialistically."[4]

In this way Bultmann applied an external norm to the myth. In the myth no distinction is made between cosmology and anthropology.[5] Bultmann's distinction gives the impression that one could separate the anthropology from the mythological-cosmological language in terms of which it was expressed; as if there were an underlying anthropology which was expressed, somewhat inadequately, in this mythological language, i.e., in terms of the cosmology. In fact, however, there was no understanding but that which actually occurred in the mythological language itself. The anthropology was conceived of as man in his world, and thus at the same time as cosmology.

Bultmann's existentialist interpretation, thus, should be understood as his reinterpretation of what he understands the New Testament to have brought to expression, or, to put it more precisely, which occurred in the New Testament mythological expressions. A major objection against this reinterpretation is that the existentialist language of Martin Heidegger's *Sein und Zeit*, which Bultmann used in his execution of it, tended to limit, if not what could be understood of that which Jesus and the New Testament writers brought to expression in their mythological language, then certainly what could be reinterpreted.

---

[1] Cf. the previous footnote.

[2] Cf. *Kyrios Christos*, Göttingen: Vandenhoeck und Ruprecht, 1913; 2nd revised ed., 1921; 5th ed., 1965; Eng. tr. by John Steely, Nashville, New York: Abingdon Press, 1970; also *Die Religion des Judentums im späthellinistischen Zeitalter*, 1903; 3rd ed. edited by Hugo Gressmann 1925; 4th ed. Tübingen: J. C. B. Mohr (Paul Siebeck), 1965.

[3] "Neues Testament und Mythologie," *KuM.* I (cf. above, p. 2, footnote 1), 1st ed., p. 23; subs. eds., p. 22; Eng. tr., p. 10.

[4] *Ad loc.*

[5] The best example in the New Testament may be the Philippians hymn (Phil. 2 : 6–11) in which the process of redemption is described entirely cosmologically. Man is never even mentioned in the hymn, except to say that the redeemer took on the human form.

C. The Significance of the Person of Jesus
for his own Proclamation

As has been indicated above[1], Bultmann has consistently maintained that according to the New Testament "'faith' as the conduct
of the new true life was not only *present* since a particular time ...,
but ... that 'faith' only became a *possibility* since a particular time,
and indeed as a result of an *event*, i.e., the Christ event."[2] "The
question is *not* whether the nature of man could have been discovered without the New Testament, for, in fact, it was not discovered without the New Testament. Modern philosophy would not
have existed if it had not been for the New Testament, Luther and
Kierkegaard."[3] Thus he could also say in connection with the theology of Paul that "in accordance with the origin of the theological
understanding in faith, ... man before the revelation of *pistis* was
described by Paul as he became visible through faith."[4]

Of great importance for us in this first part concerning the teaching
of Jesus is the fact that Bultmann does not include the teaching of
Jesus in the theology of the New Testament. So explicitly in the
first sentence of his *Theologie des Neuen Testaments*. "*The proclamation of Jesus* belongs with the presuppositions of the theology of the
N.T., and is not a part of this (theology) itself."[5] This distinction
between the teaching of Jesus and the early Christian proclamation
is diminished in two ways. First, Bultmann himself states with
regard to the message of Jesus: "Basically, thus, *he himself in his
person is the 'sign of the time.'*"[6] "*He in his person signifies the
demand for decision* in asfar as his call is God's final word before the
end, and, as such, calls to decision."[7] Thus, he could also say:
"Jesus' call to decision implies a Christology ...,"[8] a statement of
considerable significance for what has come to be known as the

---

[1] In the stating of the problem, pp. 1–5.
[2] "Neues Testament und Mythologie," *KuM*. I, 1st ed., p. 33; subs. eds.,
p. 31; Eng. tr., p. 22.
[3] *Op. cit.*, 1st ed., p. 37; subs. eds., p. 35; Eng. tr., p. 26.
[4] *Theologie des Neuen Testaments* (cf. above, p. 24, footnote 1), p. 192;
Eng. tr., p. 191.
[5] P. 1; Eng. tr., p. 3.
[6] *Theologie*, p. 8; Eng., tr. p. 9.
[7] *Ad loc.*
[8] *Theologie*, p. 46; Eng. tr., p. 43; cf. also *Glauben und Verstehen*, Tübingen:
J. C. B. Mohr (Paul Siebeck), vol. I, 1933; 4th ed., 1961, pp. 204, 266;
furthermore, *Das Verhältnis der urchristlichen Christusbotschaft zum histori-*

"new quest for the historical Jesus."[1] Secondly, Bultmann has responded positively to Herbert Braun's statement that notwithstanding the variability of the New Testament Christology and the absence of any Christology whatsoever in the proclamation of Jesus, the understanding of man was the same for Jesus, Paul and John.[2] "By reducing the intention of the various kerygmatic forms ... to the self-understanding of man before God," Braun "overcomes the question of historical continuity and replaces it with that of the constancy."[3]

The implication of Braun's position is that it recognizes that the New Testament understanding of man is already present in the proclamation of Jesus, contrary to Bultmann's statements that the proclamation of Jesus belongs with the presuppositions of the theology of the New Testament, and that "faith" as the conduct of the new true life was not only present since a particular time, but also only became a possibility since a particular time, and indeed as a result of an event, i.e., the Christ event, referred to above.[4] It should be noted, however, that Braun has consistently maintained that the New Testament understanding of man was not handed down historically. This is evident in the fact that this understanding was

---

schen Jesus, SAH., phil.-hist. Klasse, Jg. 1930, 3. Abh., Heibelberg: Carl Winter-Universitätsverlag, 1960, p. 16; Eng. tr., "The Primitive Christian Kerygma and the Historical Jesus" in Carl Braaten (ed.), *The Historical Jesus and the Kerygmatic Christ. Essays on the Quest of the Historical Jesus*, New York: Abingdon Press, 1964, p. 28.

[1] Most specifically Hans Conzelmann, who refers to it as an indirect Christology. Cf. above, p. 24, footnote 2, also "Zur Methode der Leben-Jesu-Forschung," *Zeitschrift für Theologie und Kirche*, 56 (1959), Beiheft 1, pp. 2–13, specifically p. 6; "Jesus von Nazareth und der Glaube an den Auferstandenen," *Der historische Jesus und der kerygmatische Christus*, edited by H. Ristow and K. Matthiae, Berlin: Evangelische Verlagsanstalt, 1961, pp. 188–199, specifically p. 198. So also Fuchs, who, however, substitutes Bultmann's statement with: Jesus' *conduct* implies a Christology. *Gesammelte Aufsätze* II, (cf. above, p. 20, footnote 7), p. 185, footnote 36, cf. also p. 403; Eng. tr., p. 189. Conzelmann's concept of an indirect Christology is criticized by Erich Dinkler, "Petrusbekenntnis und Satanswort," *Zeit und Geschichte. Dankesgabe an Rudolf Bultmann zum 80. Geburtstag*, edited by Erich Dinkler, Tübingen: J. C. B. Mohr (Paul Siebeck), 1964, pp. 127–153, specifically p. 151, footnote 79.

[2] "Der Sinn der neutestamentlichen Christologie," *Zeitschrift für Theologie und Kirche* 54 (1957), pp. 341–377; now in *Gesammelte Studien zum Neuen Testament und seiner Umwelt*, Tübingen: J. C. B. Mohr (Paul Siebeck), 1962, 2nd ed., 1967, pp. 243–282, specifically pp. 268f., and 275f.

[3] *Das Verhältnis*, p. 21; Eng. tr., p. 36.

[4] Cf., p. 44.

expressed without a Christology in the proclamation of Jesus, and in differing Christological formulations in Paul and John,[1] i.e., the Christology was subject to variation even though the anthropology remained constant.

Bultmann's acceptance of Braun's interpretation does not affect his insistence that the understanding *of the New Testament* is that authentic existence is possible only as a response to the proclamation of Christ, but it does mean that *in fact* authentic existence as conceived of by the New Testament was possible independent of the Christian proclamation, namely, in response to the ministry of Jesus—which is a piece of criticism of the New Testament Christological understanding from the point of view of the ministry of Jesus. According to Braun, however, authentic existence was realized *only* there in addition to its being a response to the proclamation of Christ. In a considerable part of his work he attempted to determine what the distinctive character of the New Testament understanding of man was, including the understanding of man in the ministry of Jesus, in contrast with that of its environment,[2] and concluded that it was precisely the characteristics of the human self-understanding of Jesus, Paul, and John which remained constant, which also distinguished them from their environment, namely, that it was the person who stood with empty hands to whom the grace of God was offered.[3]

The two ways in which Bultmann's distinction between the teaching of Jesus and the early Christian proclamation is softened should be distinguished, i.e., respectively, by way of the implied Christology, and by the acceptance of the concept of the constancy of the human self-understanding notwithstanding the variability of its expression. In terms of the former, the explicit Christology of the New Testament proclamation is understood to have been grounded in the Christology which was implicit in the ministry of Jesus, and

---

[1] Cf., particularly, *op. cit.*, pp. 268f., 272, 276.

[2] So in *Radikalismus* (cf. above, p. 27 footnote 1), vol. II; *Qumran und das Neue Testament* (cf. above, p. 27 footnote 1), and in most of the articles collected in his *Gesammelte Studien*. Cf. also my article "Herbert Braun's Quest for what is essentially Christian," *Journal of the American Academy of Religion*, 35 (1967), pp. 350–361.

[3] "Der Sinn der neutestamentlichen Christologie," *Gesammelte Studien*, pp. 243–282, specifically, pp. 248f., 268, 271f., 274; cf. "Die Bedeutung der Qumranfunde für das Verständnis Jesu von Nazareth," *Gesammelte Studien*, pp. 86–99, specifically pp. 97f.

thus, ultimately in the person of Jesus himself. If it can be shown
that the person of Jesus was equally important for his own ministry
as he was for the early Christian proclamation, the claim of the latter
proclamation that authentic existence was possible only in response
to the proclamation of Christ would be substantiated by the
ministry of Jesus.

Braun's procedure is almost the exact opposite. It is true that by
distinguishing between the explicit Christology of the early Christian
proclamation and what he called Christology as encounter ("Christologie als Anrede")[1] he is able to discern a certain agreement between the early Christian proclamation in the sense of the latter, and
the message of Jesus. Furthermore, according to him, the New
Testament understanding is that authentic existence is always
realized in response to a proclamation, whether it be that of Jesus,
Paul, or John.[2] Thus, he can state that in the confession of the
believer he is conscious of the fundamental equality between what
he experiences and what has taken place in relation to Jesus, and
thus, the fact that the new self-understanding expressed in his
confession comes to him from beyond himself.[3] Note, furthermore,
his statement that in "an entire layer of the New Testament, i.e., the
oldest stage of the synoptic tradition" the *"extra nos*, the event
character of the grace of God comes to expression simply by the fact
that Jesus of Nazareth speaks and acts as he does, without the
authorization of this speaking and acting by particular Christological affirmations in the narrower sense (pre-existence, atoning death,
exaltation)."[4] Thus, James M. Robinson could conclude: "Although
no explicit Christology is present with Jesus, Braun finds the material connection between Jesus and the church in the paradoxical
grace, or in the Christology as encounter, which justifies the reference to Jesus in the kerygma."[5] The question is on what basis
this justification is recognized. There is a certain justification in the
fact, referred to above, that the believer is aware of the fundamental
equality between what he experiences and what has taken place in
relation to Jesus.

---

[1] "Der Sinn der neutestamentlichen Christologie," *Gesammelte Studien*, p.
246.
[2] *Op. cit.*, pp. 276f.
[3] *Op. cit.*, p. 282.
[4] *Op. cit.*, p. 246.
[5] *Kerygma und historischer Jesus*, 1st ed., p. 27; 2nd ed., p. 44.

But for Braun the self-understanding implied in the Christology as encounter is not grounded in the Christological claim itself. Rather, the Christological claim is justified by the type of understanding which comes to expression in it, and in so far as this understanding remains constant in the ministry of Jesus and in a particular Christology, the latter is justified in co-ordinating itself with Jesus. What is primary for the reasoning based on the concept of an implied Christology is secondary for Braun who points out that a Christology can give expression to contrary self-understandings without differing in any other respect. Thus, although Käsemann is probably correct in insisting that what is "the 'most constant' in the Christian anthropology of the believer" is "the element of belonging to Christ ('das Moment der Christuszugehörigkeit'),"[1] this is an almost meaningless constancy since it applies to practically everything which calls itself Christian.

D. The ontological Grounding of the Message of Jesus

Braun's concept of the constancy of the self-understanding, notwithstanding the variability of the Christology, does not have to mean that there must have been an *underlying* anthropology which came to expression in the various Christological formulations, but it does raise the question concerning the ontological grounding of the anthropology which came to existence in these formulations. Braun has given no explicit indication where he thinks this grounding is to be found, except in a general way, namely, in man's relation to his fellowmen. So, e.g., in the assertion that the sustenance and duty which is determinative for the New Testament understanding of man is not encountered from the universe, but from one's fellowman, and"... also the word of proclamation and the act of love reaches me ... from (my) fellow-man."[2] But in a more specific way as far as the New Testament is concerned, his work does indicate where this grounding should be sought, namely, in that which made it possible for the same understanding of man to come to expression in Jesus, Paul and John, without its having been handed

---

[1] "Sackgassen im Streit um den historischen Jesus," *Exegetische Versuche und Besinnungen*, vol. II, p. 44; Eng. tr., p. 38. Cf. Braun's response to Käsemann, *Gesammelte Studien*, 2nd ed., pp. 348–350.

[2] "Die Problematik einer Theologie des Neuen Testaments," *Gesammelte Studien*, p. 341; Eng. tr. by Jack Sanders, "The Problem of a New Testament Theology," *Journal for Theology and the Church*, 1 (1965), p. 183.

down historically from the one to the other. However, Braun does
not indicate what made this possible.

For the reasoning based on an implied Christology in the ministry of Jesus, the New Testament understanding of man is
conceived of as having been grounded in Jesus himself. His person,
thus, remains essential for the Christian understanding of man. So
explicitly Käsemann: "The point is not whether he (i.e., Jesus) was
one Jew or *one* Christian among others, but that this Jew, according
to the combined witness of Christianity, is the founder and con-
summator of faith, the archetype of obedience, the new Adam, and
as such not the presupposition,[1] but the center of the New Testament."[2] Käsemann is aware that his concern in this regard is subject to the suspicion of being apologetic, but is not afraid to state
openly: "... I consider this apologetic as essential, or do not retain
the courage to call my understanding of existence Christian."[3] This
is a perfectly consistent position which deserves the appreciation
also of those who do not share it.

Notwithstanding the fact that Käsemann wrote this in the context of polemics against Bultmann, Bultmann himself shares this
position as far as the New Testament proclamation is concerned,
although in his case one would have to say that the ontological
grounding of the understanding is "the Christ event,"[4] rather than
Jesus himself. With this we are once more face to face with our basic
problem. How can a specifically *Christian* understanding of existence
be defended? The reasoning based on an implied Christology in the
ministry of Jesus simply shifts the problem one step backwards from
the primitive Christian proclamation to Jesus himself. The question
now becomes how the understanding of existence is grounded in
Jesus. To this Ernst Fuchs gives a clear answer: "Jesus risks
bringing to bear the will of God in such a way that he himself
appears in the place of God."[5] How this is to be understood according to Fuchs comes out clearly in his interpretation of the parable

---

[1] An apparent polemical statement against Bultmann, *Theologie des
Neuen Testaments*, p. 1; Eng. tr., p. 3.
[2] "Sackgassen im Streit um den historischen Jesus," *Exegetische Versuche
und Besinnungen*, vol. II, p. 48; Eng. tr., p. 42.
[3] *Op. cit.*, p. 51.
[4] Cf. "Neues Testament und Mythologie," *KuM*. I, 1st ed., p. 33; subs.
eds., p. 31; Eng. tr., p. 22. Cf. above, p. 37.
[5] *Gesammelte Aufsätze* II, (cf. p. 20, footnote 7, above), p. 154; Eng. tr., p. 21.

of th e prodigal son. He argues that one should not relate the father in th e parable immediately to God. Jesus defends his own conduct with the parable. "He does so because he rejects no sinner, and, it is true, justifies his conduct with the will of God." "Jesus, thus, means that just like himself, God accepts the repentent sinner."[1] Then follo ws a sentence which is undoubtedly crucial for Fuchs' conception, not only of the parables or even of the ministry of Jesus, but of the entire theological task. "Thus it is not the case that first of all the parable interprets the conduct of Jesus, although Jesus defends himself with it, but conversely, that Jesus' conduct interprets the will of God with a parable that can be read off from the conduct of Jesus."[2] The original, remarkably discerning sentence, cannot be translated adequately into English. Thus, I quote it in German as well. "Es ist also nicht so, dass erst die Parabel Jesu Verhalten erklärt, obwohl sich Jesus mit ihr verteidigt, sondern umgekehrt, Jesu Verhalten erklärt den Willen Gottes, mit einer an Jesu Verhalten ablesbaren Parabel."

Nevertheless, the question remains: How did Jesus come to it to risk enforcing the will of God in such a way that he himself appeared in the place of God? This really involves two distinguishable questions: How did Jesus know the will of God? and: From where did he derive the authority to enforce it through his conduct?

Robert Funk brought the problem into clear focus in his discussion of language, specifically what he calls the "foundational language" of the parables of Jesus, and the "primary reflective language" of Paul's letters.[3] It is, of course, more specifically the former which concerns us here. The designation "foundational language" is derived from this mode of language's characteristic of "creating a tradition, *founding* a world."[4] This mode of language "re-flects, without reflecting upon, the world,"[5] and thus is itself founded in "the world" which it re-flects. Foundational language, such as that of the parables, which re-flects the world in which it is founded should not be confused with the "primary reflective language," such

---

[1] *Op. cit.*, p. 154; Eng. tr., p. 20.

[2] *Ad loc.*

[3] Robert W. Funk, *Language, Hermeneutic and Word of God*, New York: Harper and Row, 1966, cf. pp. 232f.

[4] *Op. cit.*, p. 233. My emphasis.

[5] *Op. cit.*, p. 232.

as that of Paul's letters, which *reflects upon* the fate of the foundatio-nal language which it presupposes.[1]

The following statement then points directly to the ontological problem of language such as the foundational language of the parables of Jesus, but also the language event which occurred in his conduct. "Speech never comes to rest in itself, as though there were nothing left to be said; it is bounded only by more speech. There is never the one-to-one correlation between word and thing, or word and thought, which would be characteristic of finished language. Rather, language remains unfinished because signifying is always surpassed by the signified. Just as unspoken language, primordial discourse, precedes articulation, so it follows articulation: articula-tion is bounded by the silent word, from which it proceeds and to which it returns."[2] And then Funk focuses directly on the ontolo-gical problem: "The phenomenology of language, ... by attending to the silence which surrounds language, endeavors to refer language to what it intends and thus to discover the phenomena anew. In this process it uncovers the ontological bearings of language itself."[3]

This points to our fundamental problem. What are the phenomena to which the language of Jesus pointed? What were the ontological bearings of his language? Unfortunately it was not Funk's concern to "discover the phenomena anew" or to "uncover the ontological bearings of language itself." His main concern was with the "foun-dational" language of the parables of Jesus and the "primary reflective" language of Paul's letters. Beyond stating that this was the case, he did not concern himself with the fact that also the New Testament language was bounded by the silent word. Very specifi-cally our question is what world was re-flected in the language of the ministry of Jesus?

The problem of the authority of Jesus, and specifically of the "ontological bearings" of his language, to use Funk's phrase, is evaded, if not ignored by Eberhard Jüngel[4] with his view that it was the Kingdom of God ("die Gottesherrschaft") in which the authority of Jesus was grounded. So, e.g., in the headings of section 17 and 18 of his book: "The Kingdom of God as the authorizing Power of the

---

[1] Cf. *op. cit.*, p. 238, also pp. 244 and 248.
[2] *Op. cit.*, pp. 229f.
[3] *Op. cit.*, p. 234.
[4] *Paulus und Jesus*, Tübingen: J. C. B. Mohr (Paul Siebeck), 1962, 2nd ed. 1964.

Proclamation of Jesus," and "The Kingdom of God as the authorizing Power of the Demand of Jesus."

This would not be the case if he does not in turn ground the
Kingdom of God in the language of Jesus, specifically of the parables.
So, e.g., in his thesis for the interpretation of the parables: "The
Kingdom comes to expression in the parables *as* parables. The
parables of Jesus articulate the Kingdom of God as parables."[1]
This is formulated even more precisely in the following: "... the
parables of Jesus are language events in which that which is articu-
lated in them is *completely* there, in the fact that it is there *as* parable."[2] Here language is turned back into itself. Contrast this with the
discerning statements of Funk, quoted more fully above: "Speech
never comes to rest in itself, as though there were nothing more to
be said ...," and "... articulation is bounded by the silent word,
from which it proceeds and to which it returns."[3] This is not to deny
the validity of Robinson's statement that the "eschatological
meaningfulness ... comes with, indeed comes *as*, the language of
the parables;" that in the debate concerning futuristic eschatology,
realized eschatology, etc. the "material role of language itself in the
actualizing of God's reign was overlooked,"[4] as long as sight is not
lost of the fact that the parable as "language event" functions "to
expose the truth of the situation, to *show up* the situation as it truly
is."[5]

E. JESUS AND THE SECT OF JOHN THE BAPTIST
(MT. 11 : 4–19)

Mt. 11 : 2 Now John, hearing in prison of the works of Jesus, sending
through his disciples, said to him: [3]You are the coming one? or should we
expect another? [4]And replying Jesus said to them: Having gone, an-
nounce to John what you see and hear: [5]Blind see, and lame persons walk,
lepers are purified, and deaf men hear, and dead men are raised and to
poor people good news is proclaimed: [6]And blessed is he who is not
scandalized by me.

---

[1] *Op. cit.*, 2nd ed., p. 135.

[2] *Op. cit.*, p. 138.

[3] *Op. cit.*, pp. 229f., cf. above, p. 44

[4] James M. Robinson, "Jesus' Parables as God Happening", in *Jesus and
the Historian. Written in Honor of Ernest Cadman Colwell*, ed. by F. Thomas
Trotter, Philadelphia: The Westminster Press, 1968, p. 143. My emphasis
in both cases.

[5] *Op. cit.*, p. 142. My emphasis.

[7]These having gone Jesus began to tell the crowds concerning John: What did you go out into the desert to look at? A reed moved by the wind? [8]But what did you go out to see? A man clothed in soft things? Behold, those who wear soft things are in the houses of Kings! [9]But for what did you go out? To see a prophet? Yes, I say to you, and more than a prophet! [10]He is the one concerning whom it is written:

> Behold I send my angel in front of you,
> who will prepare your way before you.

[11]I say to you, none greater arose among those born of women than John the Baptist. Nevertheless, the least in the Kingdom of the heavens is greater than he.
[12]And since the days of John the Baptist until now, the Kingdom of heavens is violated, and the violators ravage it.
[13]For all the prophets and the Law prophesied until John the Baptist, [14]and if you are willing to accept, he is Elijah who will come. [15]He who has ears, listen!
[16]And with what will I compare this generation? It is like children sitting in the marketplace who call to the others, [17]saying:

> We played the flute to you and you did not dance,
> we wailed and you did not mourn.

[18]For John came neither eating nor drinking, and they said: He is possessed; [19]the Son of Man came eating and drinking, and they said: Look, a gluttonous man and a drinker, a friend of publicans and sinners; and: wisdom will be justified by her works.

Ernst Fuchs indicates that an answer to the question concerning the ontological grounding of the ministry of Jesus should be sought in his relationship to John the Baptist. He points out that it is essential to recognize that the decision demanded by the proclamation of Jesus was "simply the echo of that other decision which Jesus himself had made. We have to understand Jesus' conduct as also determined by a decision, and therefore, can infer what he himself did from what he demands."[1] This decision came for Jesus in the face of the death of the Baptist. "... for Jesus there was of necessity a question similar to that of his disciples after (his) death. Jesus, after all, experienced the violent death of the Baptist."[2] Without a doubt, through his baptism he had identified himself with the urgency of the eschatological judgment as expressed by the

---

[1] *Gesammelte Aufsätze* II, p. 157; Eng. tr., p. 23.
[2] *Ad loc.*

Baptist. Thus, after the death of the latter, he had to decide what this death meant to him. As the tradition behind Mt. 11 shows "Jesus not only continued the activity of the Baptist, but even radicalized it. However, he could not radicalize the conduct of the Baptist in the direction of the proclamation of judgment, since there was nothing (in this) that could have been further radicalized. (Cf. Mt. 11 : 11a, par. Lk. 7 : 28a). Jesus could only conceive the *time* of the Kingdom of God in a new way, i.e., he could attempt to make the time of the Kingdom his own."[1]

Fuchs identifies the correct place where an answer to our question is to be found, but it is insufficient to say that according to the tradition behind Mt. 11 it was the conception of the *time* of the Kingdom which distinguished the proclamation of Jesus from that of the Baptist. The question is how Jesus came to conceive of the time of the Kingdom differently. This could hardly have been simply because he considered it necessary to radicalize the proclamation of the Baptist. There must have been a reason why he considered this necessary.

According to the tradition of Mt. 11 what distinguished Jesus from the Baptist was the fact that the latter "came neither eating not drinking" whereas Jesus "came eating and drinking." (Mt. 11 : 18f., par. Lk. 7 : 33f.). This difference may very well have been due to a difference in conception between the Baptist and Jesus concerning the time of the Kingdom. As much as the Baptist's asceticism was a preparation for the coming of the Kingdom, Jesus' participation in life's pleasures was a celebration of its presence. The fact that the saying refers to the "coming" of Jesus may indicate that its present form is a product of the Hellenistic church, but that does not exclude its having been originally a saying of the Palestinian church with which it interpreted, not necessarily correctly,[2] the possibly authentic parable of Jesus (Mt. 11 : 16f., par. Lk.

---

[1] *Op. cit.*, p. 158; Eng. tr., p. 23.

[2] Contrary to Jeremias, *op. cit.*, pp. (139–141), 160–162; Eng. tr., pp. 160–162. He concluded, probably correctly, that with the parable Jesus (or some other author) told his hearers that they were "exactly like these domineering and intolerant children who reproach their playmates for being spoilsports because they did not want to 'dance to their tune.'" Pp. (140), 161; Eng. tr., pp. 161f. However, for his assumption that the interpretation correctly identifies the original setting of the parable, cf. pp. (140f.), 161f.; Eng. tr., p. 162f., there is insufficient evidence.

7 : 31f.) with accurate memory of the difference between Jesus and the Baptist.[1]

It should be noted that the expression of the distinction between Jesus and the Baptist in this passage does not separate them but affirms their solidarity.[2] The way in which this distinction in conjuction with the solidarity was conceived becomes clear in Mt. 11 : 10f., par. Lk. 7 : 27f. According to this tradition, which on occasion probably caused early Christians considerable embarrassment,[3] Jesus indeed proclaimed John the Baptist as the final eschatological figure before the actual coming of the Kingdom of God, who was surpassed only by those who no longer stood at the threshold of the Kingdom as the Baptist had done, but actually participated in it.

This understanding of the Baptist is expressed even more strongly in Mt. 11 : 12f., cf. Lk. 16 : 16. The original order of the two sayings in Matthew may be indicated by the single saying in Luke, namely, first the saying about the prophets and the Law (Mt. 11 : 13) and then the one about the violence suffered by the Kingdom of God (Mt. 11 : 12). The form of the sayings, however, may be more original in Matthew. Originally, thus, the combined two sayings announced that the period of the prophets and the Law ended with the Baptist, who initiated a new period in which the Kingdom of God was threatened with violence. Although the Kingdom had not actually come with the Baptist, he was already closely associated with it. According to these sayings it was John the Baptist who marked the beginning of the new age.[4]

---

[1] Cf. Bultmann, *Geschichte der synoptischen Tradition*, pp. 164, 177f., 186; Eng. tr., pp. 152f., 164f., 172.

[2] So Bultmann, *op. cit.*, p. 177; Eng. tr., p. 164.

[3] Because of the use Baptist disciples made of it in anti-Christian polemics, such as is recorded in the Pseudo-Clementine, *Recogn.* I 60: "And behold, one of the disciples of John affirmed John to have been the Christ, and not Jesus, inasmuch as, he said, even Jesus himself pronounced John to be greater than all men and prophets."

[4] So Käsemann, "Das Problem des historischen Jesus," *Exegetische Versuche und Besinnungen*, vol. I, p. 210; Eng. tr., "The Problem of the Historical Jesus," *Essays on New Testament Themes*, pp. 42f.; also Robinson, *The New Quest of the Historical Jesus*, pp. 116–121, *Kerygma und historischer Jesus*, pp. 143–147; 2nd ed., pp. 208–213.

The Lukan order does not exclude the Baptist as initiator of the new period of salvation, as Jüngel suggests, unless one chooses part of the Lukan reading as he does: "The Law and the prophets were until John. From then on the Kingdom suffered violence and men of violence take it by force." *op. cit.*, p. 191. It is Luke's *apo tote* = "from then on" which places the Baptist back in the previous period. Cf. Jüngel, *op. cit.*, pp. 191f.

The contents of Mt. 11 : 12f. convinced Käsemann of their authenticity. "Who else but Jesus could look back in this way on the concluded period of salvation of the Old Testament, (and) not degrade the Baptist to a precursor, as the entire Christian community and the entire N.T. did, but included him on his side and letting him initiate the new eon, something (which was) abominable to subsequent Christian ears."[1] Bultmann considers Mt. 11 : 7–11a as authentic—with verse 10, however, a Christian interpolation—but not verse 11b and verses 12f., because of the degrading of the Baptist which he believes is expressed in these verses.[2] But if the degrading of the Baptist occurs only in Lk. 16 : 16, where it is used to give expression to Luke's understanding of history,[3] Bultmann's objection against the authenticity of Mt. 11 : 12f. is removed.[4] And verse 11b is not an expression of the degrading of the Baptist, but of an actual change in the situation after the time of the Baptist as Jesus perceived it, as will be argued below in connection with the discussion of Mt. 11 : 4–6.[5] It is not difficult to recognize that the Baptist could have made it possible for Jesus to perceive that it was the poor who were blessed because theirs was the Kingdom of God (Lk. 5 : 20b, cf. Mt. 5 : 3), since it was through self-imposed poverty that the Baptist prepared himself for the coming Kingdom of God.

Jüngel points out that if Käsemann is correct in arguing that according to Mt. 11 : 12f. the new age had already started with John the Baptist, the question becomes how Jesus could still have understood the Kingdom as a phenomenon of the future, as Käsemann also assumes.[6] If John already marked the beginning of the new age then "Jesus already looks back to the *olam haba* in terms of which

---

[1] *Ad. loc.*

[2] *Geschichte der synoptischen Tradition*, pp. 177f.; Eng. tr., pp. 164f., cf. *Das Verhältnis der urchristlichen Christusbotschaft zum historischen Jesus*, p. 16; Eng. tr. (cf. above, p. 37 footnote 8), p. 29.

[3] Cf. Hans Conzelmann, *Die Mitte der Zeit*, Tübingen: J. C. B. Mohr (Paul Siebeck), 4th ed., 1962, p. 17; Eng. tr. by G. Buswell, *The Theology of St. Luke*, London: Faber and Faber, New York: Harper and Bros., 1960, p. 23.

[4] Cf. Robinson, *The New Quest of the Historical Jesus*, p. 117, footnote 1; *Kerygma und historischer Jesus*, p. 144, footnote 2; 2nd ed., p. 210, footnote 32.

[5] So also Jüngel, *op. cit.*, p. 174, footnote 5, but with a different understanding, namely, that according to Jesus the Baptist did belong in the previous period with the Law and the prophets. Cf. *op. cit.*, pp. 191, 192f.

[6] Jüngel, *op. cit.*, p. 192; cf. Käsemann, *op. cit.*, p. 212.

he speaks of the Kingdom."[1] "How can Jesus say that (the Kingdom) already realizes itself since John the Baptist *heōs arti* in such
a way that it is already being opposed, when (in fact) it realizes itself only from *now* on (*ap arti*)."[2] Thus Jüngel concludes that "as
long as these logical contradictions burden Käsemann's exegesis,"
he "prefers" the interpretation that "not Jesus, but Matthew (or the
primitive Church) placed the Baptist at the 'beginning of the new
age.' Jesus combined the coming age as the, for the present, distant
future, with the near future of the Kingdom of God in such a way
that the *power* of this Kingdom of God 'pioneered a way' for itself
in the conduct of Jesus."[3]

Contrary to Jüngel, however, it is suggested here that, in view
of the available evidence, consistency should be found in the opposite
direction, namely, by recognizing that Jesus perceived the Kingdom
of God as having already come.

For this Mt. 11 : 4–6, par. Lk. 7 : 22f. offers almost conclusive
evidence. The question in connection with these verses is how Mt.
11 : 5, par. relates to Mt. 11 : 6, par. Bultmann, who considers
these verses as authentic,[4] points out that the saying (Mt. 11 : 5,
par.) "actually only wants to depict the blessed end time, which
Jesus now perceives as breaking in, with the colours of (Deutero-)
Isaiah, without the necessity of relating the individual statements to
individual events that already occurred," and that this is contrary
to the present context according to which the saying, as a reply to
the question of the Baptist, "must be a reference to (Jesus') miracles,
as Luke clearly indicates with his addition of verses 20f."[5] It may
be not insignificant that Matthew apparently understood the saying
as a reference to the miracles of the disciples as well (cf. esp.
10 : 8f.).[6] Thus Bultmann rejects the understanding of the saying as

---

[1] Jüngel, *op. cit.*, pp. 192f.
[2] *Op. cit.*, pp. 192f.
[3] *Op. cit.*, p. 193.
[4] *Geschichte der synoptischen Tradition*, pp. 135f., and explicitly on p. 163;
Eng. tr., pp. 128f., and p. 151.
[5] *Op. cit.*, p. 22; Eng. tr., p. 23.
[6] Heinz Joachim Held points out that "Matthew's own formulation in
11 : 2, *ta erga tou Christou* (= 'Christ' works of Jesus), refers not only to the
activity of Jesus, but obviously also to the activity with which the disciples
had been charged in the mission speech which, according to Mt. 10 : 7f.,
corresponds exactly with that of Jesus. But then the reference of Jesus to
'that which you see and hear' (Mt. 11 : 4f.) intends not only his own proclamation in word and deed, but also that of his disciples." "Matthäus als

originally referring to the messianic role of Jesus. "The Jews did indeed expect miracles in the messianic age (Mt. 11 : 2–6 remains in this framework), but they did not conceive of the figure of the Messiah as a worker of miracles."[1] But since the saying alone "has no point," and thus, must have belonged with Mt. 11 : 6, par. from the beginning, he does consider it as a reference to the proclamation of Jesus in which "his messianic consciousness would indeed come to expression."[2] And so Bultmann in the end makes a contradictory statement when he writes in connection with the original meaning of Mt. 11 : 5f., par.: "... one can observe—say in Jesus' exorcisms—the new age already breaking in,"[3] only to add once more that it was the evangelists who narrowed down the meaning, as Q had already done: "The depiction refers to the activity of Jesus (i.e.), to his miracles, which legitimize him as the Messiah."[4]

This contradiction can be avoided if one interprets Mt. 11 : 6, par. from verse 5, par., rather than the other way around as Bultmann does, i.e., Jesus based his own activity (verse 6) on the fact that the Kingdom of God had already come. In this way it would be possible to avoid contradicting the meaning of verse 5, par. as originally established by Bultmann. He is correct in pointing out that Mt. 11 : 5, par. has no point by itself, but its meaning hardly becomes clear even if it is read in conjunction with only verse 6, par., as Bultmann's own difficulties in interpretation indicate. However, it does become clear when it is read in conjunction with verse 4, par., namely, as a reply to a query from the Baptist—of course not the present Christologizing question (verses 2f., par.), which is obviously a formulation of the early Church.[5] Nevertheless, if verses 5f., par. were originally a reply to a query of the Baptist, as verse 4, par. suggests, it would have made it very easy for the early church to place the Christologically formulated question in the mouth of the Baptist.

Originally then, Mt. 11 : 5f., par. was a reply of Jesus to a query of the Baptist through some of his disciples, among whom Jesus

---

Interpret der Wundergeschichten," *Überlieferung und Auslegung im Matthäus-Evangelium* (cf. above, p. 15 footnote 3), pp. 239f.; Eng. tr., p. 252.

[1] *Op. cit.*, p. 275, cf. p. 135; Eng. tr., p. 257, cf. p. 128.
[2] *Op. cit.*, p. 135, cf. pp. 115, 136; Eng. tr., p. 128, cf. pp. 110, 129.
[3] *Op. cit.*, p. 136; Eng. tr., p. 129.
[4] *Ad loc.*
[5] Cf. Bultmann, *op. cit.*, p. 22; Eng. tr., p. 23.

himself belonged earlier, and maybe, in some sense, even at that time. In his reply, Jesus defended his conduct (verse 6) by pointing to the fact that the Kingdom of God had already come, which he substantiated by referring to what was taking place around him (verse 5). With his defense, Jesus, at the same time, vividly exhorted the Baptist and his closer disciples to join him in the step he had taken: "Blessed is he who is not scandalized by me!" (verse 6, par.). The step Jesus had taken must indeed have been offensive to the ascetic Baptist and his more loyal followers (cf. the tradition of Mk. 2 : 18–22). The saying of Mt. 11 : 6, par., thus, does not "imply a Christology." Concretely, but gently, Jesus challenged the Baptist and his disciples with the step he had taken, namely, his acceptance of the fact that the Kingdom of God had come, and his celebration of its presence. Note the increased force of the commendation of the Baptist in verses 7–11a when this meaning of verse 6 is presupposed. The contrast between the sayings of verses 5f. and 7–11a is once more present in the single saying of verses 18f. with which the section is concluded.

Jesus' proclamation reflected the world in which he lived, or, more accurately, his proclamation was the way in which he experienced his world. But then it is not necessary to assume that he came to the realization that the Kingdom of God had come by an act of will, i.e., by a decision, whether it was in the face of the violent death of the Baptist,[1] or as a result of some other event. And, in particular, there is no need to assume that "Jesus (risked) it to enforce the will of God in such a way that he himself (appeared) in the place of God."[2]

Jesus did not consider himself, but the Baptist as the one who had initiated the Kingdom of God. He also did not suggest that he in his person was evidence that the Kingdom had actually come, but that observable signs revealed this, such as the miracles that were taking place, and these were almost certainly not limited to himself and his disciples. His message was *euangelion* = "proclamation of good news" in the true sense, namely, an invitation to participate in the Kingdom of God. "To poor people good news is proclaimed" (Mt. 11 : 5, par.). Apparently it was the *am ha'ares*, the people of the land, and not the elite, who responded to the announcement, i.e., with whom Jesus made contact. That this was correct Jesus argued with parables such as the great feast (Mt. 22 : 1–10, par.).

---

[1] So Fuchs, *Gesammelte Aufsätze* II, p. 157; Eng. tr., pp. 22f.
[2] Fuchs, *op. cit.*, p. 154; Eng. tr., p. 21; cf. above, p. 42.

This, of course, still does not explain how he had come to believe that the Kingdom of God had actually come. In looking for an answer to this question, the following facts should be borne in mind. Jesus, who, through baptism, had become a member of a sect which withdrew itself from what it considered the defiled world in expectation of the coming of the Kingdom of God, now became confident that the expected Kingdom had already come, a fact which he celebrated by living a life directly contrary to the asceticism he must have previously shared with the sect. As Mt. 11 : 5f. shows, his non-ascetic life and his confidence that the Kingdom had come, apparently belonged together.

There does not seem to have been much evidence in the historical situation of Jesus to convince him that the Kingdom had actually come, except for the miracles to which he referred (Mt. 11 : 5, par.). But even if there had been such evidence, the mere fact that he believed that the Kingdom had come as such would hardly explain why he gave up his previous ascetic withdrawal from the world in preparation for its coming, for the directly opposite embracing of that same world. From the point of view of the Baptist sect, to be sure, the fact that the Kingdom of God had come could hardly have been justification for the conduct of Jesus. His behaviour must have been appalling to them, and their controversy with him is quite understandable. The question is rather why they even continued to bother about him. For some reason they took him seriously enough to argue with him, and Jesus, in turn, apparently retained considerable regard for the Baptist as texts such as Mt. 11 : 7–11, and 18f. reveal.

In the debates which ensued between the sect and Jesus after he had given up his ascetic way of life, Jesus was apparently called upon, or felt himself called upon, to answer for his conduct. He did this by claiming that the Kingdom of God had come. But then it appears that the coming of the Kingdom of God may not have been the motivation for his conduct, but his justification of it. The unity of his ministry is to be found, not in his belief that the Kingdom had come, but in his acceptance of his world, and his attraction to the people of the world, the *am ha'ares*.

The fundamental question thus shifts from how Jesus came to believe that the Kingdom of God had come, to why he had given up the ascetic withdrawal from the world into the circle of the Baptist sect, for an almost diametrically opposite acceptance of the world.

The answer, if it could be found, may very well be a psychological one. There have been many people through the ages—and there will certainly be many more—who gave up an intended ascetic life simply because they could not take it, and because they were too much attracted by a more wordly life.

The reason why Jesus may have made this change, thus, could well be considered trivial, although simply wanting to be with people the way Jesus did, does not have to be considered trivial. However, his significance does not lie in the fact that, as many others through the ages, he gave up an ascetic life for a wordly one, but in the fact that he felt himself called upon to justify this step, in the beginning, to his one-time fellow members of the Baptist sect and to their leader, but subsequently to more diverse groups with differing points of view. What may be even more important is the fact that he probably had to justify it to himself. This would have demanded even more serious answers to the questions with which he was confronted. In all of this the dialectical tension of his ministry manifested itself, because he had to reconcile the Kingdom of God which was sacred and which he had previously urgently awaited, with the unholy world with which he now identified himself and in which he was forced to believe the Kingdom had arrived. His continued confrontation with the pious ensured the continuation of the tension, and thus also, the continued demand of reconciliation. In this way the ministry of Jesus became, in a sense, a continuous realization of a theology out of the ghetto of religious exclusiveness.

CONCLUSION

The tradition of Mk. 4 : 33 still reflects the original sense in which Jesus made use of parables, namely, as a means of being readily understandable to all who heard him. His proclamation was anything but an esoteric teaching, such as Mk. 4 : 11f. suggests. It had been intended to be generally understandable, even to his adversaries. Furthermore, he did not proclaim himself, but in his teaching tried to interpret man's situation in the world. The validity of his teaching depended on the effectiveness with which he disclosed man's situation in his world.

A stringent application of the existing criteria for determining authentic tradition of Jesus led to the conclusion that the futuristic eschatology tradition in the synoptic gospels could not be considered as characteristic of the ministry of Jesus since this eschatology was part of Jewish environment out of which Jesus came. Furthermore it appeared that there was no way of reliably reconstructing the min-- istry or teaching of Jesus since all that is certain about the so-called criterion of discontinuity, is the discontinuity itself. It is not a reliable criterion for determining whether or not tradition actually originated from Jesus. Thus, it was suggested that a more profitable procedure would be, rather than try to rediscover the teaching of Jesus, to attempt to understand the discontinuity which came to expression in connection with his ministry. In such an attempt the emphasis shifts from the authority and person of Jesus, to the understanding of man in his world which came to expression in his ministry.

Here the question of the ontological grounding of the ministry of Jesus, and specifically of his teaching or language, became important. An answer to this question is suggested by the tradition of Mt. 11 : 4–19, concerning the relationship of Jesus to the sect of John the Baptist. A discussion of this tradition suggests that the ministry of Jesus was grounded in the fact that after his initial membership in the ascetic sect, he gave up his withdrawal from the sinful world, returning to an outright worldly existence. His language, thus, could be understood as a product of the tension between the sacredness of the Kingdom of God for which he previously prepared by participating in the asceticism of the Baptist sect, and the secularity of his existence in a world which was considered defiled by the Baptist sect, but to which he returned and in which he believed the Kingdom of God had arrived. The language of Jesus was grounded in his experience of man's situation in the world, as the articulation of this situation, to which it also referred back as the source of its authority.

As has been indicated above, the primitive church responded to the proclamation of Jesus by confessing that he acted with divine authority. This was expressed especially by honoring him with various "Christological" titles. In this way the emphasis shifted from Jesus' disclosure of man's situation in the world to a dependence on his person. This meant that the understanding of man once more became dependent on a religious predisposition, i.e., towards the person of Jesus. This emphasis, which was characteristic of New Testament Christianity, found its most extreme expression in the Gospel of John in the New Testament, where a correct understanding was understood to depend not on man's natural ability, but on a special gift of God which was reserved for only some. Nevertheless, there are at least two instances where the typical exclusiveness of the New Testament proclamation is broken by a more fundamental understanding of faith, namely, in the description of the last judgment in Mt. 25 : 31–46, and in Paul's interpretation of the faith of Abraham as the type of Christian faith in Rom. 4. To these matters we now direct our attention.

PART TWO

THE CLAIM OF ABSOLUTENESS IN THE
CHRISTOLOGY OF THE NEW TESTAMENT

INTRODUCTION

The Exclusiveness of the Christological Understanding

It has been argued in Part I that Jesus challenged his hearers not to take offense in him, *not for his person*, but for the hermeneutic of reality which his ministry represented, and with which he identified himself. So especially in the tradition of Mt. 11 : 4–6.[1] No faith commitment was required of them as a prerequisite for understanding him. All that was required was the ability to recognize the validity of his teaching as an articulation of their world. This contrasts radically with a Christological understanding such as that of the Fourth Gospel, according to which it was precisely the person of the redeemer that was decisive. So, e.g., in John 3 : 16, "For thus God loved the world, that he gave his beloved Son, in order that *everyone who believes in him* will not perish, but have eternal life,"[2] and 5 : 25, "... the hour is coming and now is when the dead *will hear the voice of the Son of God, and those who hear* shall live."

But even hearing his voice, i.e., acceptance of him as the one who was sent by the Father, was dependent on a divinely given predisposition. So, e.g., explicitly in 3 : 27, "No person is capable of

---

[1] Cf. above, pp. 50ff.

[2] Cf., e.g., C. K. Barrett, *The Gospel according to St. John*, London: SPCK., 1955. "...while God loves the world (as is stated in this verse) his love only becomes effective among those who believe in Christ." (P. 180). Slightly exaggerated may be the formulation of Walter Bauer: "In any case the world loved by God existed for him only of the believers and the Son's giving of himself." *Das Johannesevangelium. Handbuch zum Neuen Testament*, Tübingen: J. C. B. Mohr (Paul Siebeck), 1925, p. 54.

In his existentialist interpretation of the Gospel, Bultmann has almost interpreted the exclusiveness away by clarifying its meaning. So, e.g., in connection with this verse. "That then, is the real miracle, that in faith the exaltation of the Son of Man is believed ... Faith in (the sending of the Son) is at the same time faith in his exaltation, because only he who, by overcoming the stumbling block of humility, recognizes in the death (of Jesus) his exaltation, can recognize in (him) the Son who was sent by the Father. And conversely, faith in the exalted one (verse 15) affirms, at the same time his humbling (verse 16)." *Das Evangelium des Johannes. Kritisch-exegetischer Kommentar über das Neue Testament*, Göttingen: Vandenhoeck und Ruprecht 12th ed., p. 111.

accepting anything unless it is given to him from heaven;"[1] 6: 44, "No one is capable of coming to me if the Father who sent me does not draw him;" and 6 : 25, "... no one is capable of coming to me unless it is given to him from the Father."[2]

Of course, the Johannine Christology is also a cypher for a specific, i.e., gnostic understanding of the world, and the dependence of the acceptance of Jesus on a divinely given predisposition, a cypher for the fact that there were some who did and others who did not accept the Johannine understanding of man's situation in the world. What is significant for us here is the fact that what was real in this case was not the world of Jesus and his hearers. The validity of the teaching of the Johannine Jesus, as well as the ability of his hearers to recognize him, was derived from beyond the world, i.e., from the Father in heaven who sent Jesus, and who gave the ability to recognize him only to those whom he chose. According to this understanding, what was real, was not of this world. This world, in fact, stood in opposition to what was real, i.e., with heaven.

John understood salvation to have been grounded outside of this world, even if he understood the gnostic statement that "unless one is born from above, he is not capable of seeing the Kingdom of God" (3 : 3c) in the sense of a new birth through the Spirit (cf. verses 4–8), and not in the original sense of the limitation to those who were of heavenly origin.[3] The latter understanding is still clearly reflected also in 3 : 13, "No one ascends into heaven, except he who descended from heaven."[4] The difference between John and his gnostic source(s) in this is the fact that the source(s) had it that the

---

[1] Cf., however, the interpretation of this verse by R. Schnackenburg, who suggests that *didonai ek* should not be understood, as is usually the case, in contrast with *lambanein*, but should be understood in the sense of "it has been given him to do something." The sense of the verse would then be: "Jesus could not have drawn so many people to himself, had God not given him the power to do so. To that which he 'took' for himself, God helped him." *Das Johannesevangelium, I Teil, Einleitung und Kommentar zu Kap. 1–4* Freiburg–Basel–Wien: Herder, 1965, pp. 452f.

[2] Cf., e.g., Barrett, *op. cit.*, pp. 245, 252, and also in connection with 3 : 16, "...it is made clear that men in general do not, and cannot, love God (3 : 19; 5 : 42; 8 : 42)." (P. 180).

[3] Cf. Bultmann in connection with 3 : 13. "...there is an ascent into heaven only for those who originate from heaven, for the *anōthen gennētheis*, only for the pre-existent souls." (*op. cit.*, p. 107).

[4] So, e.g., Bultmann. Cf. the previous footnote. The interpreting desi gnation, "the Son of Man," was probably added by the evangelist. So Bultma nn, *op. cit.*, p. 107, footnote 4. According to him, if "Son of Man" was alrea dy

distinction between those who were capable of salvation and those who were not, depended on the heavenly origin of the former which the latter lacked, whereas John understood this distinction to have been brought about by a divine intervention through the Spirit, without which salvation would not have been possible for anybody.[1] But for both, salvation, i.e., recognition of the revealer who came from outside, depended on capabilities which also came from without of this world.

As has been suggested above, these gnostic-Johannine concepts can in fact be understood as cyphers for this-worldly realities, i.e., the negative gnostic attitude towards the world, and variations of self-assertion in the face of disbelief. But by articulating it in this way all further discussion is cut off. Apparently the validity of cutting off argument in this way can be taken for granted from a confessional Christological point of view. So, e.g., Barrett in connection with 6 : 44. "The complaint is pointless and the dispute in which the Jews are engaged must be fruitless; it cannot lead them to come to Jesus. Only the direct act of God—not the mere resolution of some problem—can effect this." "Hence Jesus merely reiterates the truth and does not seek to establish it by force of argument; those whom the Father gives to him will be drawn to him, with or without argument, and they will not be cast out; those whom the Father does not give, will not come."[2]

The hearers of Jesus were not dependent on special other-worldly capabilities. Their ability to understand his parables as the articulation of their world, which meant both liberation and judgment, is the diametrical opposite of the special ability which John understood to have been given to only certain of Jesus' hearers. John, of course, also understood the words of Jesus to have functioned immediately as salvation and as judgment. So, e.g., in 3 : 18. "He who

---

part of the original saying, it would have had the gnostic sense "that the totality of pre-existent souls compose the *huios tou anthrōpou*, the primeval man who landed out of the world of light in the darkness." (*ad. loc.*).

[1] Cf. Bultmann. "...man as he is, is excluded from salvation, from the sphere of God. For him, as he is, it is no possibility." (*op. cit.*, p. 95).

[2] *Op. cit.*, p. 245. Barrett's reference to Mk. 10 : 23–27 as a synoptic parallel is misplaced. For one thing, argument is not simply cut off in this passage, but, more important, it does not refer to a distinction between those who are drawn to Christ and those who are not, but expresses confidence in the incomprehensible mercy of God in the face of man's inability to truly fulfill

believes in him (i.e., in the Son) is not judged, but he who does not believe is already judged, because he did not believe in the name of the beloved Son of God." Salvation meant to recognize his voice. When man, trapped in this world, which is the realm of death,[1] hears, i.e., recognizes the voice of the Son of God, he will live. (5 : 25). But whereas it was the recognition of *the reality of this world* which meant liberation and judgment for the hearers of Jesus, it was the recognition of the reality of *what was not of this world*, which meant salvation and condemnation in John's gospel. Possibly one could formulate it most simply by saying that Jesus affirmed that this world was what was real, whereas the Johannine understanding was that what was real was not of this world.

And whereas Jesus mediated liberation and judgment merely by articulating the reality of his world as he experienced it in his teaching, the Johannine Jesus himself became the sole source of salvation for mankind. Thus, he could say: "I am the way and the truth and life. No one comes to the Father, except through me." (14 : 6). This conception of Jesus as the exclusive bringer of salvation is also brought to expression, not only in explicit statements such as Acts 4 : 12, "... salvation is in no-one else for there is no other name under the heavens which was given to men through which we should be saved," but in every case where he is proclaimed as the one who specifically brought about salvation, which is to say, it is typical of the Christology of the New Testament.

Only in a few instances in the New Testament, this absoluteness of the Christological claim in the sense of an absoluteness of salvation through the confession of Christ, is qualified by an understanding in the sense of the absoluteness of the concept of existence for which Christ stands, namely, the description of the Last Judgment in Mt. 25 : 31–46, and Paul's understanding of Abraham as the example of Christian faith in Rom. 4. To these we now turn our attention.

---

[1] Cf. Bultmann, who, of course, decyphers this, i.e., interprets it existentialistically as follows: "...the *nekroi* to whom reference is made, are, of course, the people of the *kosmos* who live an inauthentic life, because they do not know the *alēthinon phōs* (1:9) and the life which he spends." (*op. cit.*, p. 195).

CHAPTER THREE

MT. 25 : 31–46. CHRISTIANITY AS HUMANISM

Mt. 25 : 31 And when the Son of Man would have come in his glory and all the angels with him, then he will sit on the throne of his glory. ³²And assembled before him will be all the peoples, and he will separate them from each other, as the shepherd separates the sheep from the goats, ³³and he will place the sheep on his right, and the goats on (his) left.

³⁴Then will the king say to those on his right: Come, you blessed ones of my father, inherit the kingdom prepared for you since the creation of the world. ³⁵For I hungered and you gave me to eat; I thirsted and you let me drink; I was a stranger and you invited me; ³⁶naked and you clothed me; I was sick and you cared for me; I was in prison and you visited me.

³⁷Then the righteous answered him, saying: Sir, when did we see you hunger and fed you, or thirst and let you drink? ³⁸And when did we see you a stranger and invited you, or naked and clothed you? ³⁹And when did we see you sick, or in prison, and visited you?

⁴⁰And in reply the king said to them: Truly I tell you, inasmuch as you did it to one of these brothers of mine, of the least (of them), you did it to me.

⁴¹Then he also said to those on his left: Go away from me you who are accursed to the eternal fire which is prepared by the devil and his angels. ⁴²For I was hungry and you did not give me to eat; I thirsted and you did not let me drink; ⁴³a stranger and you did not invite me; naked and you did not clothe me; sick and in prison and you did not care for me.

⁴⁴Then also they answered, saying: Sir, when did we see you hunger or thirst or a stranger or naked or sick or in prison, and did not serve you?

⁴⁵Then he answered them, saying: Truly, I tell you, inasmuch as you did not do it to one of these, of the least (of them), you did not do it to me.

⁴⁶And these went away to eternal punishment, but the righteous to eternal salvation.

A. Problems in the Interpretation of the Passage

This passage is not a parable, but, as has been widely recognized, and for a long time,[1] a *description* of the Last Judgment, which

---

[1] Cf., e.g., Jülicher, *op. cit.* (cf. above, p. 11, footnote 1), vol. I, e.g., p. 272, footnote 1, p. 302, etc.; Joh. Weiss, *Die Schriften des Neuen Testaments neu übersetzt und für die Gegenwart erklärt*, edited by Joh. Weiss, vol. I, *Die drei älteren Evangelien. Die Apostelgeschichte*, Göttingen: Vandenhoeck und

functions as an exhortation. Joh. Weiss nevertheless suggests that it was possibly based on an original parable.[1] That the present form of the description in its entirety is in any case not original is indicated by the tension between "the Son of Man" in verse 31, and the "king" in verses 34 and 40. Jeremias suggests that Matthew is responsible for this tension by having introduced the reference to the Son of Man in verse 31. "... it is very similar to Mt. 16 : 17, and the Son of Man sitting on the throne of glory is to be found only in Matthew (25 : 31; 19 : 21)."[2]

Contrary to the assumtion of Th. H. Robinson—"(the passage's) general form and meaning are too familiar to need comment, for they are self-explanatory"[3]—the interpretation of the passage is highly controversial and uncertain. The uncertainty arises particularly in connection with the question whether the recipients of the acts of relief were disciples,[4] or people in general who were in need,[5]

Ruprecht, 1906, p. 360; E. Klostermann, *Das Matthäusevangelium. Handbuch zum Neuen Testament*, Tübingen: J. C. B. Mohr (Paul Siebeck), 3rd ed. 1938, p. 204; Jeremias, *op. cit.*, (cf. above, p. 11, footnote 1), pp. (172), 204; Eng. tr., p. 206; F. Filson, *A Commentary on the Gospel according to St. Matthew*, London: Adam and Charles Black, 1960, p. 266.

Deplorable exceptions are S. E. Johnson, "The Gospel according to St. Matthew," *The Interpreter's Bible*, New York, Nashville: Abingdon Press, vol. VII, 1951, p. 562; and Th. H. Robinson, *The Gospel of Matthew. The Moffat New Testament Commentary*, London: Hodder and Stoughton, 1951, p. 208.

[1] *Op. cit.*, p. 360; cf., however, Klostermann, "...not a parable—also not a former one..." (*op. cit.*, p. 204).

[2] *Op. cit.*, pp. (172), 204; Eng. tr., p. 206.

[3] *Op. cit.*, p. 208.

[4] So, e.g., B. Weiss, *Das Matthäus-Evangelium, H. A. W. Meyers Kritisch-exegetischer Kommentar über das Neue Testament*, Göttingen: Vandenhoeck und Ruprecht, 8th ed., 1890, p. 434; J. Wellhausen, *Das Evangelium Matthaei* Berlin: Georg Reimer, 1904, p. 134; Theodore Zahn, *Das Evangelium des Matthäus*, Leipzig: A. Deichert'sche Verlagsbuchhandlung, 1905, p. 675; Klostermann, *op. cit.*, p. 207, cf. pp. 204f.

[5] So, e.g., Joh. Weiss points out that the interpretation according to which non-Christians "are to be judged only according to whether they acted in a decent way or not to Christians, attributes an intolerable Christian pride which almost borders on fanaticism to our evangelist," *op. cit.*, p. 360; A. Schlatter, *Der Evangelist Matthäus*, Stuttgart: Calwer Vereinsbuchhandlung, 1933, pp. 725f., Jeremias, *op. cit.*, pp. (173f.), 205; Eng. tr., p. 207; Filson, *op. cit.*, pp. 266f.; Pierre Bonnard, *L'Évangile Selon Saint Matthieu. Commentaire du Nouveau Testament*, Neuchatel: Delachoux et Niestlé, 1963, p. 367.

and whether the persons judged are Christians,[1] specifically non-Christians,[2] or people in general.[3]

All of these questions arise out of another single question: What is the relation between the acts of relief and the confession of Christ? Also here the interpretations differ. So, for example, Klostermann argues that the absence of phrases such as "in my name" (Mk. 9 : 37, par.s) or "in the name of a disciple" (Mt. 10 : 42), which would have revealed the specifically Christian character of the acts of relief, may be due to the fact that the passage was concerned solely with Christians,[4] and thus could be presupposed. Joh. Weiss, on the other hand, emphasized that the actions were precisely not motivated by a conscious relationship to Christ.[5] To the contrary, "... characteristic is precisely that the righteous performed their good deeds to the poor and suffering *without* thinking about Jesus. Whoever, like the compassionate Samaritan, acts wherever he sees suffering ... should know that with that he proved his love for Jesus personally." "What is done in love, Jesus wants to consider as if it is done for his sake, but it is precisely not expected that it be done consciously for Jesus' sake or in his name."[6] Highly relevant for the present inquiry is Weiss' next statement. "This is a solemn sanctioning of what is referred to from ecclesiastical side, unfortunately frequently with deprecation, as 'humanitarian,' and it includes a contradiction of the opinion that an act of love is perfect only when it is done in the name of Jesus."[7]

The interpretation of Weiss seems to be softened somewhat by the fact that he considers the passage to be intended within what is already a Christian context.[8] Thus, the acts of relief are not un-

---

[1] So, e.g., Wellhausen, *ad loc.*; Joh. Weiss, *op. cit.*, pp. 360f.; Klostermann, *op. cit.*, p. 207.

[2] So, e.g., Zahn, *op. cit.*, pp. 675f.; Jeremias, *op. cit.*, pp. (175f.), 206f.; Eng. tr., pp. 208f.; Bonnard, *op. cit.*, p. 367, who, however, points out that in Matthew it serves as an exhortation for Christians.

[3] So, e.g., Schlatter, *op. cit.*, pp. 725f.; Filson, *op. cit.*, pp. 266f.

[4] *Op. cit.*, p. 207.

[5] *Op. cit.*, p. 178. So also Schlatter, *op. cit.*, p. 726. Klostermann specifically rejects the interpretation of Weiss. (*ad loc.*)

[6] Joh. Weiss, *ad loc.*

[7] *Ad loc.* It should be noted, however, that although Weiss appreciates this passage—cf. his reference to the "herrliche Idee, die in der Mitte steht, V. 35-40" (p. 360)—he considers it onesided since "we can find in other sayings of Jesus himself that he attached at least equal weight to other things, (i.e.), purity of heart, truthfulness, humility." (*op. cit.*, p. 361).

[8] *Op. cit.*, p. 360.

derstood as unqualified humanitarian acts, but in the sense of Mt.
7 : 21, "Not everyone who calls me Lord, Lord, will enter into the
Kingdom of the heavens, but he who does the will of my father who
is in the heavens."[1] According to this saying the confession of Christ
is not sufficient. It has to be coordinated with the doing of the will of
God.[2] Weiss, however, also radicalizes the understanding of the latter saying. "(Jesus) declares the 'saying Lord, Lord' worthless
compared with the *doing* of the will of God."[3] And so also in connection with our passage: "... also here it is presupposed that the
persons concerned are disciples—they call him 'Lord'—but not
that, not a 'conscious' relation to his person, not even to mention,
a correct confession, is decisive, but the *act of love*."[4]

It cannot be half-hearted radicality, but, we must assume, the
result of his concern for the meaning of the text which made Weiss
narrow it down, insisting that the passage, "like everything preceding (it), was written for the Christian community, as admonition
and sharpening of the conscience. Every Christian could belong with
the goats, everyone to the sheep. There can be no doubt that the
consideration was mainly Christians."[5]

The basic difficulty with the text becomes evident in the interpretation of Bonnard. Contrary to Weiss and others he does not
assume that the description itself was originally intended within a
Christian context, but with Jeremias and others he considers it to
have been concerned with the judgment of the nations. "... verse
32 (*panta ta ethnē*) shows that it is concerned above all with the
judgment of the nations."[6] But, very much like Weiss, he argues
that "it is undeniable that Matthew, in the context of chapters 24
and 25, applied it to 'Christian disciples' of his church. They are the
disciples of 24 : 3 who are exhorted to merciful vigilance with regard
to all the disinherited."[7] However, with this Bonnard shifts the
center of focus of the passage from the moral qualities of the agents
to a concern for all who are in need of help. "The Matthaean ethic,
thus, is universalist with regard to its object (service to all people),

---

[1] *Op. cit.*, p. 361.
[2] Cf., e.g., Schlatter, *op. cit.*, pp. 258f.
[3] *Op. cit.*, p. 361.
[4] *Ad loc.*
[5] *Op. cit.*, p. 360.
[6] *Op. cit.*, p. 367.
[7] *Op. cit.*, p. 367.

but particular with regard to its agents (the Christians). One may add, however, that it is not *reserved* for Christians ...".[1] This is good, but not the intention of the passage.

Nevertheless, Bonnard may have recognized the basic difficulty with the interpretation of the text, namely, the tension between what appears to be its universalist context, and its apparent function as an admonition for Christians. This suggests that a solution of the problems in connection with the interpretation of the passage may be found if this tension could be resolved.

B. The meaning of the Description

The tension between the designation "Son of Man" in verse 31 and "king" in verses 34 and 40 is resolved by the assumption, with Jeremias,[2] that Matthew introduced the former designation. The question then is how much of the present passage was added by Matthew with the introduction of the title "Son of Man." The entire introductory scene (verses 31–33) suggests itself, the placing of "the sheep on his right, and the goats on his left" (verse 33) serving as a transition to the original description in which those who were found righteous were at the right hand of the King, and those who were condemned, at his left. The description itself, however, appears to be original. It was not based on some other source, e.g., an original parable.[3] This suggestion is supported by the following considerations.

There is a clear shift in the scene from verses 31–33 to verses 34ff. The introduction is impersonal, general; the judgment scene, personal, existential. This in itself, of course, does not make the former, possibly with some alterations, impossible as the original introduction to the latter. The present actual judgment scene must originally have had some form of an introduction. It could not have commenced with verse 34. Nevertheless, it has no necessary connection with its present introduction. Already Wellhausen remarked in connection with the assembled nations: "(Their presence is) only grandiose background. No further thought is given to them."[4]

---

[1] *Ad loc.*
[2] *Op. cit.*, pp. (172), 204; Eng. tr., p. 206, cf. above, p. 64.
[3] Contrary to Joh. Weiss, *op. cit.*, p. 360; cf. above, p. 64.
[4] *Op. cit.* p. 134.

The solution that the present introductory scene is secondary also absorbs many of the conflicting points in the various interpretations of the passage, by resolving the tension which appears to be the basic cause of these conflicting interpretations, namely, the conflict between its universalist context and its function as a Christian exhortation. Thus, Bonnard would be correct in arguing that Matthew used the description to exhort "'Christian disciples' of his church,"[1] but the universalist context which he assumes for the description itself on the basis of "all the nations" of verse 32,[2] apparently was not part of it originally. The tension between the universalist context and the specifically Christian exhortation appears to be due to an accident, namely, as a result of the introduction by Matthew of the description with the apocalyptic scenery. This placed the description in a universalist context, although Matthew probably did not specifically intend to expand the interpretation in this way.

That the actual description of the judgment was not intended in a universalist sense is also suggested by the Jewish parallel from the Midrash quoted by Jeremias. In Tann. 15 : 9 God says to Israel: "My children, when you gave the poor (something) to eat, I reckon it for you in this way, as if you had given me (something) to eat."[3] So closely parallel are these passages that the mere elimination of only two short phrases—*tou patros* = "of the father" in verse 31, and *tōn adelphōn moy* = "of my brothers" in verse 40[4]—could leave Mt. 25 : 34–46 a Jewish description in which God figures as the central figure. In that case it would be a simple variant of the Midrash passage. It would only be difficult to conceive of the close identification of the king with those who are afflicted if it was a Jewish description in which God was understood to be the king. "Inasmuch as you did it to one of these, of the least of them, *you did it to me*" (verse 40). Note that the Midrash passage has "... I reckon it for you ..., *as if* you had given me to eat." Nevertheless, the closeness of the parallels are expressed accurately in Jeremias' formulation that in Mt. 25 : 31–46 "Jesus has stepped in the place of God."[5]

---

[1] *Op. cit.*, p. 367.

[2] *Ad loc.*

[3] Quoted after Jeremias, *op. cit.*, pp. (173), 205; Eng. tr., p. 207.

[4] God could hardly have been conceived of as referring to afflicted human beings as his brothers.

[5] *Op. cit.*, pp. (173), 205; Eng. tr., p. 207.

The description, thus, as is the case with the Midrash passage, is to be understood as an exhortation which emphasized humanitarian acts as a decisive basis for the final Judgment. As such it was intended for fellow believers, but not for them distinctively. The question whether non-believers would be judged similarly, apparently, in neither of the passages entered into the consideration.

The only remaining question of significance for the interpretation of the original judgment scene is in connection with the phrase "my brothers" in verse 40. It is correct, but not sufficient, to argue, with Jeremias, that a "comparison with verse 45 shows that the disciples are not meant with the *adelphoi* ..., but all oppressed and suffering."[1] The question is what purpose the phrase serves in the text. Standing in front of *tōn elachistōn* = "of the least," it has emphasis, which could be of considerable significance. It could have one of two meanings. Either it gives expression to the close relationship which is established in the description between Jesus and those who are afflicted, or it was intended as a limitation of those who effectively received the acts of relief to disciples in the service of Christ. In the latter case the phrase would have to be understood as an addition which was made after the description was supplied with its present introduction. It presupposes that the passage was understood, no longer as an exhortation of Christians, but as the announcement that aid to disciples in service of Christ would be the basis for the judgment of non-Christians. In this case the absence of the phrase in a few manuscripts[2] may be of some significance.

If, on the other hand, *tōn adelphōn moy* = "of my brothers" was part of the original description, or was added as an expression of the close relationship established between Jesus and those who suffer affliction, the phrase would in fact express this relationship in a less radical way than would be the case without it. Without the phrase a full practical identity between Jesus and those who are afflicted is established: "... inasmuch as you did it to one of these, of the least (of them), *you did it to me.*" The phrase "my brothers" draws attention to a relationship, i.e., between Jesus and his "brothers," which motivates the judgment. This tends to mute the otherwise unqualified identity, even if it is only to a very slight degree. This slight difference is easily recognized when one considers the

---

[1] Jeremias, *ad loc.*
[2] B* 1424ff[2] Cl.

fact that a Jewish original in which God figured as the central person, i.e., the king,[1] would be better conceivable if a phrase such as "my children" occurred as the appropriate original in the case of God, in the place of the present "my brothers" for Christ.

C. Matthew's Understanding of the Passage

Matthew probably understood the description in a sense similar to that of the Midrash passage, as an exhortation to fellow believers to aid their fellowmen when they are in need, but with Christ taking the place of God. It is not correct to take it with Joh. Weiss as a parallel to Mt. 7 : 21.[2] The latter saying, at the conclusion of the Sermon on the Mount, is to be understood within the context of Matthew's legalism which dominates the "Sermon."[3] (Cf. 5 : 17–19). The "doing the will of my Father who is in the heavens" is meant in the sense of obedience to the Law.

The saying of Mt. 7 : 21 also does not declare the "'saying Lord, Lord' worthless compared with the *doing* of the will of God,"[4] but emphasizes that the confession of Christ in itself is insufficient— "not *everyone* who calls me Lord, Lord will enter into the kingdom of the heavens." It must be co-ordinated with the doing of the will of God.[5] This saying has a close parallel in Matthew's understanding of the saying: "Many are called but few elected" (22 : 14) with which he concluded his combination of the parables of the great feast and the man without a wedding garment (22 : 1–13). Matthew understood the latter as a reference to the member of the Christian community who does not wear the wedding garment of obedience to the Law, i.e., of doing the will of God.[6]

In our passage, rather than insist on obedience to the Law, the true intention of Christian obedience to it is interpreted in a sense

---

[1] Cf., above, pp. 68f.

[2] *Op. cit.*, p. 361, cf. above, p. 66.

[3] So, e.g., Barth: "With that Matthew supplied the Sermon on the Mount with brackets in 5:17ff., that are clearly directed against antinomians, and thus understand the entire Sermon on the Mount in the context of this question concerning the Law." *op. cit.*, (cf. above, p. 15, footnote 3), p. 69; Eng. tr., p. 74.

[4] Contra Joh. Weiss, *op. cit.*, p. 361.

[5] Cf., e.g., Schlatter, *op. cit.*, pp. 258f.

[6] For an analysis of the passage, cf. Jeremias, *op. cit.*, pp. (154ff), 186ff.; Eng. tr., pp. 187ff.

closely similar to that of the parable of the compassionate Samaritan, to which Weiss correctly also refers as a parallel,[1] i.e., as an active concern for one's fellowman. Mt. 25 : 31–46, thus, is not a parallel to 7 : 21, but rather a supplement to it which interprets what it means to do "the will of my father who is in the heavens." Thus, also, it is unfounded to use Mt. 7 : 21 as a parallel by means of which our passage can be interpreted as if it teaches that it is "not (the calling Jesus 'Lord'), not a conscious relation to his person, not even to mention, a correct confession, (that) is decisive, but the *act of love*."[2] Matthew understood the description much more simply as an exhortation to Christians to come to the aid of their fellowmen in need, as a practical realization of their adherence to Christ. Those who failed to do so, failed this realization, and thus, rendered useless their confession of Christ. But the passage does not polemize against the confession of Christ, neither in the original description, nor in Matthew's application of it. It simply interprets what such a confession means in practice.

Nevertheless, Weiss correctly argued that the point of the passage was that the acts of relief were performed, or left undone, *without* Jesus in mind.[3] This is made clear by the questions of those who were judged. (Verses 38f., and 44). They were unaware that their acts of help to their fellowmen, or the absence of these, were in fact done to Jesus, or refused him.

D. The Significance of the Description

This passage then does not seem to be as profitable for our inquiry as one may have hoped. It remains within the framework of the confession of Christ as an exhortation of fellow believers. There is no indication that persons outside the Christian community even come into consideration. The passage does not suggest that a non-believer who comes to the aid of his fellowmen in need will be justified. This problem remains outside the field of vision of the passage, appearing to be part of it only as a result of the apocalyptic setting of the Matthaean introduction. In this regard the parable of the compassionate Samaritan appears to be more radical, its field of vision not

---

[1] *Op. cit.*, p. 361.

[2] Joh. Weiss, *ad loc.*

[3] *Op. cit.*, p. 178; so also Schlatter, *op. cit.*, p. 726, but contrary to Klostermann, *op. cit.*, p. 207. Cf. above, pp. 65f.

having been narrowed by the context of the confession of Christ.

Nevertheless, the passage opens up a wider perspective within Christianity with the point that the acts of relief were not performed with Jesus in mind. The decisive question is not what the text *says*, but what it *does*. What happens in primitive Christianity with this text? Here it becomes important to focus once more on the setting of the description, having in mind specifically the question: What is interpreted by what?

If the setting of the description had been the judgment of non-Christians, or even of people in general, it would have to be understood, notwithstanding the best of intentions, as a piece of Christian imperialism. In that case it justifies what are understood to be unqualified acts of human relief by interpreting them as having been done to persons who are to be identified with Christ. The person of Christ, thus, would serve to interpret what were considered unqualified acts of aid to fellow human beings in such a way that *they would in fact be crypto-Christian acts*. In this sense the passage really answers the question how non-Christians who deserve justification can be justified without contradicting the absoluteness of Christ and the confession of him. Implicit in this understanding is the fact that these persons are justified because with their deeds they in fact also confessed Christ. From a non-Christian point of view this can be considered only as an expression of Christian condescension. The narrowness of an exclusiveness of Christ is expanded to an inclusiveness, with which the bonds of a confession are not broken, but expanded.

Further consideration also reveals that, contrary to what seems to have been the case at first, the text is more radical as a Christian exhortation than it would have been if it was concerned with acts of non-Christians. In this case, acts that are as such non-Christian, even though performed by Christians—they were not done in the name of Christ—are used to interpret the meaning of the confession of Christ. Thus, although it is true that acts by non-Christians do not enter into the Christian perspective of the passage, it is all the more remarkable that it was the non-Christian *acts* of Christians, one could say secular acts, or, with Weiss, refer to them with the ecclesiastical expression of deprecation as humanitarian acts,[1] which disclose what it means to be a Christian.

---

[1] *Op. cit.*, p. 178.

The phrase "of my brothers" in verse 40 tones this down somewhat, as has been indicated above.[1] With this phrase there is a certain Christian justification for the persons who came to the aid of those who were in need in the fact that the latter were the "brothers" of Jesus. In this case too, the acts are interpreted as after all Christian, i.e., with the "brotherhood" of Christ. Nevertheless, whether this phrase was an original part of the description or a subsequent addition to it (still understood as a Christian exhortation), the toning down effected by it was probably not intentional. The phrase was probably an expression of the intimate relationship between Jesus and those who suffer affliction, which was understood to have been established by the description.

Thus the passage may appear less radical in one sense, from a non-Christian point of view, inasmuch as acts of non-Christians do not even come into consideration. But in reality, as seen from its Christian point of view, it is for that very reason all the more radical since it lets non-Christian acts interpret what the Christian confession really means. With that, in a very radical way, it allowed itself to be let in on a dialogue with the world, by allowing itself to be confronted *and interpreted by worldly acts*. Something similar happened in Paul's understanding of the function of Abraham's faith in Rom. 4, in contrast with the Christian imperialism of Gal. 3.

---

[1] P. 70.

CHAPTER FOUR

THE SIGNIFICANCE OF ABRAHAM FOR THE CHRISTIAN FAITH

INTRODUCTION

It is the relationship of the faith of Abraham and the faith in Christ which is of particular interest for us in Gal. 3 and Rom. 4. Our interpretation of these two chapters, thus, will focus specifically on the question of this relationship. Even more specifically, our interest is in the shift which takes place in Paul's interpretation of this relationship from Gal. to Rom.

Of primary significance in both Gal. and Rom. is the fact that Paul was intent to reason that those who believe in Christ are the true children of Abraham. The point of departure for this reasoning in Gal. is 3 : 5. "He, thus, who equips you with the Spirit and works powers in you; is (he) from works of the Law or from the listening of faith?"[1] The intention is, of course, not that he who equips with

---

[1] It is not correct to assume that the missing words, which can be presupposed, but are necessary to make the sentence meaningful are *touto epoiēsen* which results in the following meaning. "He, thus, who equips etc., did he do so from the works of the Law or from the listening of faith?" So W. Bousset, "Brief an die Galater," *Die Schriften des Neuen Testaments neu übersetzt und für die Gegenwart erklärt*, ed. by J. Weiss, vol. II, *Die Briefe. Die johanneische Schriften*, Göttingen: Vandenhoeck und Ruprecht, 1907, p. 44; E. de W. Burton, *A critical and exegetical Commentary on the Epistle to the Galatians*, Edinburgh: T. and T. Clark, 5th impr. 1956, p. 151; H. Schlier, *Der Brief an die Galater. Kritisch-exegetischer Kommentar über das Neue Testament*, Göttingen: Vandenhoeck und Ruprecht, 13th ed., 1965, p. 118; P. Bonnard, *L'Épitre de Saint Paul aux Galates. Commentaire du Nouveau Testament*, Neuchatel: Delachaux et Niestlé, 1953, p. 64; R. R. Stamm, "The Epistle to the Galatians," *The Interpreter's Bible*, New York, Nashville: Abingdon Press, vol. X, 1953, p. 500; less explicitly Th. Zahn, *Der Brief des Paulus an die Galater*, Leipzig: A Deichert'sche Verlagsbuchhandlung, 2nd ed., 1907; and with a slightly different formulation, M.-J. Lagrange, "...did he act in this way because you practiced etc.," *Saint Paul. Épitre aux Galates. Études Bibliques*, Paris: J. Gabalda, 1926, pp. 61, 63. The only word that could be presupposed without difficulty, is the verb "is."

A decisive weakness with the interpretations based on the assumption of an unwritten *touto epoiēsen* is that they make verse 5 a repetition of verse 2. So, e.g., Burton, "This sentence in effect repeats the question of v. 2, and,

the Spirit and works powers, i.e., God, is "from works of the Law or from the listening of faith," but "he who equips you with the Spirit and works powers in you, is he such a one as acts in accordance with the rule of the works of the Law or in accordance with the rule of the listening of faith?"[1] With that Paul places his argument on a broader basis compared with the questions of verses 2–4 in which he appealed to the experience of his Galatian readers. Now he appeals to the author of that experience, namely, God. The next step would be to substantiate that God is such a God as he claims him to be. This he does in verses 6ff., by reference to the faith of Abraham.

This way of reasoning was intended to be particularly effective, since it placed the argumentation on a basis which Paul could assume his opponents also acepted.[2] In effect he came to grips with them on what he believed to be their own base,[3] namely, Abraham as the example of existence in faith,[4] but in such a way that he

---

like that, is doubtless to be understood as referring to the experiences of the Galatians in connection with and shortly after their conversion." P. 151. So also Zahn, *op. cit.*, p. 145; Lagrange, *op. cit.*, p. 61; Bonnard, *op. cit.*, p. 64. Schier is more cautious. Cf. *op. cit.*, p. 125. To the contrary, it should be clear that Paul now specifically shifts the attention from the Galatians to God who is the giver of that which they received (verse 5a). The reason for the above-mentioned translation may be obvious. If an *estin* is supplied, God seems to be presented as being "out of the works of the Law or out of the obedience of faith," which makes no sense. But this is not the way the verse with a presupposed *estin* has to be understood. The intention of the verse is: "He, thus, who equips you with the Spirit and works powers in you, is he such a one as acts in accordance with the rule of the works of the Law or in accordance with the rule of the listening of faith?" Cf. Rom. 3:27, where Paul distinguishes between the rule (*ho nomos*) of works and the rule of faith.

[1] Cf. the end of the previous footnote.

[2] So Ulrich Wilckens, "Zu Romer 3, 21–4, 25," *Evangelische Theologie*, 24 (1964), pp. 595f., in connection with Rom. 4, although in a somewhat different sense than will be argued below. For the rabbinic views on this point, cf. (H. Strack and) P. Billerbeck, *Kommentar zum Neuen Testament aus Talmud und Midrash*, München: C. H. Beck'sche Verlagsbuchhandlung, 2nd ed., 1954, vol. III, pp. 186–201.

[3] It is of no significance here whether or not Paul understood his opponents in Galatia correctly. What is important for us is the position he understood himself to be arguing against. For a discussion of the problem of Paul's Galatian opponents, cf. particularly Walter Schmithals, "Die Häretiker in Galatien," *Zeitschrift für die neutestamentliche Wissenschaft*, 47 (1956), pp. 25–67, now in Walter Schmithals, *Paulus und die Gnostiker*, Hamburg-Bergstedt: Herbert Reich, 1965, pp. 9–46.

[4] Cf., e.g., Billerbeck, *op. cit.*, pp. 187f., also F.-J. Leenhardt, *L'Épitre de Saint Paul aux Romains. Commentaire du Nouveau Testament*, Neuchatel: Delachaux et Niestlé, 1957, p. 67.

robbed them of this base, claiming that it could serve as a base only for his position. The final purpose of this reasoning was, of course, to reclaim his Galatian readers for "the gospel of Christ" (1 : 7, cf. 8f.). In this way Abraham became a decisive figure for Paul, and he did not surrender him again, although he was going to argue in a different way in Rom. 4 on this base supplied to him by the faith of Abraham.

Paul's interest in Abraham was motivated by something far more significant than the mere *inability* "to leave him as a crown witness for the Jewish counterposition" (Günter Klein).[1] He had a positive interest in Abraham, but this was also not because "we need the Old Testament to understand Christ" as Ulrich Wilckens argues in support of a proposition of Gerhard von Rad.[2] It is true that in Gal. 3 and Rom. 4 Paul interpreted the Christian faith from the Old Testament, specifically with the faith of Abraham, but he did not look at the Christian faith from the point of view of Abraham, or the Old Testament. Rather, looking at Abraham from the point of view of the Christian faith, he found the latter substantiated by the faith of Abraham, something he clearly did not find, e.g., with regard to Moses. (Cf. Gal. 3 : 19f.; also Rom. 10 : 5). This was a powerful argument for the Christian faith, and particularly so against what he believed to have been his Judaïzing opponents. What had probably been decisive, and conclusive, in making the discovery of the significance of Abraham's faith for the faith in Christ, was Gen. 15 : 6. This text, which is quoted in Gal. 3 : 6 and Rom. 4 : 3, except for insignificant variants, in literal agreement with the LXX, forms the point of departure of Paul's reasoning concerning the faith of Abraham in Gal. 3 and Rom. 4.[3]

Günter Klein correctly maintains (against Ulrich Wilckens) that Rom. 4 is not "a *locus classicus* for the conception of a history of salvation, but for the wholesome desacralization of a supposedly

---

[1] Günter Klein, "Römer 4 und die Idee der Heilsgeschichte," *Evangelische Theologie*, 23 (1963), p. 431; and again "Heil und Geschichte nach Römer IV," *New Testament Studies*, 13 (1966) p. 44.

[2] "Die Rechtfertigung Abrahams nach Römer 4," *Studien zur Theologie der alttestamentlichen Überlieferung*, ed. by R. Rendtorff and K. Koch, Neukirchen: Neukirchener Verlag, 1961, pp. 111f., 126f.

[3] So, e.g., Otto Michel, *Der Brief an die Römer. Kritisch-exegetischer Kommentar über das Neue Testament*, Göttingen: Vandenhoeck und Ruprecht, 12th ed., 1963, p. 115.

salvation (history) to profane history,"[1] and that the same applies to Gal. 3.[2] Nevertheless, Klein interprets these passages too much as if Paul was consciously facing up to an historical problem. "Paul has a specific interest in Abraham, which, to begin with, grew out of a consciously encountered problem, (namely), that Abraham appears to be excluded historically from the *dikaiosynē ek pisteōs*, but could not be left by Paul as a crown witness for the Jewish counter position."[3] He formulates the problem as follows. "If the possibility of experiencing the righteousness of God has a chronological point *ante quem non*, and if this is identical with the historical date of the death of Jesus, how then, one must ask, can the scriptural proof for the righteousness of God be hung up on a figure such as Abraham who is a representative of that time in which the righteousness of God could not yet be experienced?"[4] For the fact that Paul was conscious of this problem he refers to Rom. 4 : 1f. "The question what Abraham 'found,' loses much of its strangeness when one recognizes that in what precedes, Paul limited the possibility of experiencing the justification to the time *post Christum crucifixum*, but, on the other hand, (that) Abraham was considered as the prototype of the righteous in contemporary Judaism. Then only the possibility which Paul proposes hypothetically in verse 2 seems to remain: Abraham, who lived in the epoch preceding the present time of salvation..., receives his righteousness out of works, not out of faith."[5]

It is inconceivable how Paul could have experienced this as a problem if earlier, in Gal. 3 : 6, as Klein himself formulates, he quoted Gen. 15 : 6, having as his purpose "the destruction of the

---

[1] "Römer 4 und die Idee der Heilsgeschichte," p. 442; also "Heil und Geschichte nach Römer IV," p. 47. (For both, cf. above, p. 76, footnote 1.) For the controversy between him and Wilckens on this subject, cf., in addition to the above mentioned two articles, "Individualgeschichte und Weltgeschichte bei Paulus," *Evangelische Theologie* 24 (1964), pp. 126ff., and "Exegetische Probleme in Römer 3, 21-4, 25," *Evangelische Theologie*, 24 (1964); Wilckens, "Die Rechtfertigung Abrahams nach Römer 4," (cf. above, p. 76, footnote 2); "Zu Römer 3, 21-4,25" (cf. above, p. 75, footnote 2); also Leonhardt Goppelt, "Paulus und die Heilsgeschichte: Schlussfolgerungen aus Röm. IV und I. Kor. X. 1-13," *New Testament Studies* 13 (1966), pp. 31ff.

[2] Cf. "Individualgeschichte und Weltgeschichte bei Paulus," pp. 163-165.

[3] "Römer 4 und die Idee der Heilsgeschichte," p. 431; cf. "Heil und Geschichte nach Römer IV," p. 44.

[4] "Römer 4 und die Idee der Heilsgeschichte," p. 429.

[5] *Op. cit.*, p. 430.

Jewish claim of sonship of Abraham and the reclamation of Abraham as the exclusive forebear of the Christians."[1] That Abraham was justified by faith was beyond doubt for Paul as a result of Gen. 15 : 6. The question, "how ... can the scriptural proof for the righteousness of God be made to depend upon a figure such as Abraham who is a representative of that time in which the righteousness of God could not yet be experienced?"[2] did not occur to Paul, although it could legitimately be asked. Paul did not find it necessary to justify his text. Rather it serves as the basis of his reasoning in Gal. as well as in Romans. What follows the text in both cases are not justifications of it, but expositions.

But decisive and conclusive an argument as Gen. 15 : 6 evidently was for the justification by faith, Paul himself apparently did not quite know in what sense his text was to be understood, interpreting it differently in Gal. and in Rom. This underscores our understanding that he did not conclude that the text supported his position on the basis of an interpretation of it. Gen. 15 : 6 was a proof-text, which, however, he did not take for granted, apparently considering it necessary to interpret how it was to be understood, first in Gal. 3, and then again in a different way in Rom. 4, without recalling the former interpretation in the latter.

A. Gal. 3 : 6–29. Christians, in Christ, the Seed of Abraham

Gal. 3 : 2 This alone, (oh ignorant Galatians,) I wish to learn from you: From the works of the Law is it that you received the spirit, or from obedience of faith? [3]Are you so ignorant? Having made a beginning with the spirit you now bring it to completion with flesh? [4]Did you endure so much in vain?—if indeed it is in vain. [5]He, thus, who equips you with the Spirit and works powers in you; is (he) from works of the Law or from the listening of faith?

[6]As Abraham believed in God, and it was reckoned to him as righteousness. [7]Recognize then that those who are from faith, they are children of Abraham. [8]And Scripture, having foreseen that God justifies the peoples out of faith, preannounced to Abraham: Blessed in you will be all the peoples. [9]Thus, those who are from faith are blessed with the faith of Abraham.

[16]To Abraham the promises were made and to his seed. It does not say:

---

[1] "Individualgeschichte und Weltgeschichte bei Paulus," p. 148.
[2] Klein, "Römer 4 und die Idee der Heilsgeschichte," p. 429.

And to your seeds, as (speaking) about many, but as (speaking) about one: And to your seed, who is Christ. [17]This then I say: A testament that had previously been ratified by God, the Law which came three hundred and forty years later does not cancel, so as to make the promise useless. [18]For if the inheritance is from the Law, it is no longer of the promise, but to Abraham God granted it through the promise.

[26]For all of you are sons of God through faith in Christ Jesus: [27]For whosoever of you are baptized in Christ, have put on (clothed yourselves with) Christ. [28]...: For all of you are one in Christ Jesus. [29]And if you are of Christ, you are then seed of Abraham, inheritors according to the promise.

The relationship between the faith of Abraham and the faith in Christ comes to expression in Gal. specifically in 3 : 16–18, and 26–29. In essence Paul's argument is that Abraham's faith was, in a sense, faith in Christ, since the one seed in which the promise to him went into fulfilment was Christ. (The fact that Paul's rabbinic reasoning in terms of the *one* seed[1] is altogether unconvincing may be overlooked here for the sake of the argument). The relationship between the faith of Abraham and the Christian faith is not argued in terms of the identity of Christ as the object of the faith for both Abraham and the Christians, but in the sense that this relationship is determined by the fact that the latter participate, "through faith, in (the one seed) Christ Jesus" (3 : 26,[2] cf. verse 28b, also 2 : 20) in whom the promise to Abraham went into fulfilment. This "being in Christ" is realized in baptism, which is understood as a

---

[1] Cf. Bousset, *op. cit.*, (cf. above, p. 75, footnote 1), p. 47; Zahn, *op. cit.*, (cf. above, p. 75, footnote 1), pp. 166–168; Lagrange, *op. cit.*, (cf. above, p. 75, footnote 1), pp. 77–79; Schlier, *op. cit.*, (cf. above, p. 75, footnote 1), p. 146; Bonnard, *op. cit.*, (cf. above, p. 75, footnote 1), p. 71. Lagrange and Schlier both misinterpret Zahn as if he thinks of it as a reference to Isaac. The relevant sentence in Zahn, *op. cit.*, p. 166, is concerned with passages in Genesis, and is intended to establish the general principle of exclusiveness. That he too understands it as a reference to Christ is clearly indicated by the following: "...the one Christ, the son of Abraham, Isaak and Jacob (Mt. 1:1f.), is the universal heir who makes his co-inheritors all the others who are supposed to participate in the promised goods. They become it *en Christōi*," (*op. cit.*, p. 168).

[2] There is general agreement that *dia tēs pisteōs en Christōi Jēsou* = "through the faith in Christ Jesus," is not to be understood as if "in Christ Jesus" indicates the object of "the faith." "... in Christ Jesus" gives expression to the being in Christ in which the Christian participates "through the faith" in him. Christ as the object of faith is indicated by means of a genitive (e.g., Gal. 2:16,20; 3:22; Rom. 3:22,26, etc.), but also with a *pros* with acc. (Phlm. 5). So Schlier, *op. cit.*, pp. 171f.; Bonnard, *op. cit.*, p. 77; Zahn, *op. cit.*, pp. 185f., cf. also Burton, *op. cit.*, (cf. above, p. 75, footnote 1), p. 202; etc.

clothing of oneself with Christ (3 : 27).[1] Christ, thus, is understood here as "universal heir"[2] of the promise.

The relationship of Abraham to Christ and that of the Christian to him, is not the same. This is already true because, as Schlier states, whereas Abraham's faith was faith in the promise, the faith which has become possible with the obedience of Christ Jesus, is faith in the fulfilment. It is realized, fulfiled faith.[3] Schlier, however, thinks too much in terms of the structure of faith in his interpretation of Gal., thus anticipating Rom. 4. This is explicit in statements such as: "... the Galatian Christians received the Spirit through the preaching of faith. 'As also Abraham believed.' As hearers of the preaching of faith they stand in the same line with him, the believing father of Israel."[4] Also: "Sons of Abraham are those who stand with him in faith. *hoi ek pisteōs* has a comprehensive meaning: It refers to those who have in *pistis* the fundamental way of their lives, of whom the principle of life is pistic."[5] Similarly C. K. Barrett, after having correctly identified the difference between the faith of Abraham and that of the Christian believer. "Christian believers become heirs of the promise not by works of the Law, *nor by imitating Abraham's faith*, but by the faith through which they are joined to Christ. Naturally, this is not very different from the faith that Abraham had; it too rests upon the power of God to raise the dead. This leads us back to Rom. iv."[6] The second last sentence contradicts Barrett's initial correct insight, and is not drawn from Gal. but from Rom. Thus it does not "lead back to Rom. iv," because it comes from there.

In Gal. Paul does not argue in terms of the structure of faith at all, and, as has already been indicated, also not in terms of the identity of Christ as the object of faith for both Abraham and the Christian believers, although the latter is clearly understood to be

---

[1] Cf. in particular Bousset, *op. cit.*, p. 50; Albrecht Oepke, *"en," Theologisches Wörterbuch zum Neuen Testament*, (cf. p. 11, above, footnote 1), vol. 2, p. 538; Eng. tr., p. 542; also *"endyō," op. cit.*, vol. 2, p. 320; Eng. tr., p. 320. The sacramental understanding of the verse is not accepted by Burton, *op. cit.*, pp. 204–206.

[2] Schlier, *op. cit.*, p. 145; cf. also Oepke, *"en,"* p. 538: "Fundamental (for the expression) is the conception of Christ as universal person."

[3] *Op. cit.*, p. 141; cf. Bonnard, *op. cit.*, p. 70.

[4] *Op. cit.*, p. 127.

[5] *Op. cit.*, p. 128.

[6] C. K. Barrett, *From First Adam to Last*, London: Adam and Charles Black, 1962, p. 41.

the case. His reasoning in Gal. is in terms of the Christian believers' participation in Christ (3 : 26f., 29), the one seed of Abraham in whom the promise to him went into fulfilment (3 : 16), as had been intended already at the announcement of the promise (3 : 8, cf. 29). Christians, thus, have no direct relationship to Abraham. Their relationship to him is dependent on their belonging to Christ (3 : 29). Christians and Abraham are on opposite, although not opposing, but rather complimentary sides of Christ. He is the mediating point between Abraham and the peoples that are blessed in him (3 : 8, cf. 29). At the same time the meaning of Christ is understood here to be his mediation as the fulfilment of the promised blessing of the peoples to Abraham.

This is not salvation history, but eschatological to the highest degree, and thus, in a sense, directly contrary to a salvation historical understanding. The *end*, the fulfilment, was *first*, and on that basis the promise was made to Abraham. "Scripture, having foreseen that God justifies the peoples out of faith, pre-announced to Abraham: Blessed in you will be all the peoples." (3 : 8). Thus, it is completely misplaced to speak of "a *pre-evangelic* announcement of the gospel (of justification by faith),"[1] and also not correct to say, with Schlier, that it is materially in agreement with Paul's intention to say "that the gospel for the nations *began* with that promise to Abraham that he would be the blessing of the gentiles."[2] Paul's eschatological understanding here is radically anti-historical in the sense that everything that happened between the announcement of the promise and its pre-envisioned fulfilment is understood to have had no essential relationship to either. It was, so to speak, a whiling away of time, with which a lapse of time, and thus a beginning and a completion, becomes meaningless. The Law came in between, but had no power to interfere with the promise or its fulfillment (3 : 17–20), although it did serve beneficially as a "prodder,"[3] to prevent the Jews from degenerating into the state of

---

[1] Burton, *op, cit.*, p. 161. (My italicizing).

[2] *Op. cit.*, p. 130. (My italicizing).

[3] As is currently generally recognized, the Greek *paedagōgos* was not a paedagogue, i.e., a tutor or educator, but mostly a useless slave whose task it was to accompany a child to see to it that he remains obedient to the rules of behaviour set up by the head of the house. Cf., e.g., Zahn, *op. cit.*, p. 184; Schlier, *op. cit.*, pp. 168f.; Bonnard, *op. cit.*, p. 76.

"sinful gentiles" (3 : 21–25; cf. 2 : 15).[1] But when Christ came the function of the prodder was dissolved (3 : 24f., cf. 4 : 1–5). Rather than as a history of salvation from Abraham to Christ, Paul interprets this as a period in which time was, so to speak, *frozen*, both with the *proïdousa* = "fore-seeing" of scripture (3 : 9), and with the coming in between of the Law, complete with Moses and all the rest (3 : 17–25), in the period when time was being whiled away.

A completely different understanding of the relation between Abraham and the Christian believer is expressed in Romans.

B. ROM. 4. ABRAHAM'S FAITH, THE TYPE OF CHRISTIAN FAITH

Introduction

Paul's reasoning in Gal. 3 : 6–29 was polemical, having been called forth by the question whether God is such a one as acts in accordance with the rule of the works of the Law or in accordance with the rule of faith (Gal. 3 : 5). In that chapter he argued, not by interpreting the character of faith, but by trying to prove that Abraham was the forefather of those who believe in Christ and not of those who are under the Law. (Cf. particularly, 3 : 11f.). In his reasoning the character of faith does not come into consideration; neither Abraham's, nor that of the believer. For the reasoning in Gal. the *structure* of Abraham's faith was of no particular significance. The fact was that Christians *who participate in Christ*, through faith, realized in baptism, were the true descendents of Abraham. This is the way Paul interpreted his proof-text, Gen. 15 : 6, in Gal. 3 : 16f., 26–29.

That does not mean that he did not *assume* some sort of structural analogy between the faith of Abraham and the Christian faith. This was probably already given to him by the mere word "faith" it-

---

[1] Cf. Zahn, *op. cit.*, p. 184: "For a predetermined period of development, the Law had to regulate the external behaviour of Israel; to prevent it from losing itself in the unbridled heathendom by straying onto selfdetermined ways..." Questionable about Zahn's formulation is only the reference to a "(period of) *development*." That this is his intention is indicated by the conclusion of the sentence: "... (to prevent Israel) from becoming incompetent for the reception of future higher instruction, and, with that, for its essential calling." So also Bonnard, *op. cit.*, p. 74: "...Paul displays ... *the character of expectation and preparation in view of Christ* (of the role of the Law)." There is no indication of such a function of the Law here in Galatians.

self.[1] It was probably the coordination of faith and justification in Gen. 15 : 6 which suggested the text to him in the first place, but this factor never comes into consideration in his reasoning in Gal., and was also irrelevant for it. As a matter of fact, all that does come up in connection with the structure of faith reveals a difference between Abraham's faith and that of the believer, namely, Abraham's faith having been in the promise which was to have been fulfiled in his one seed, Christ, and the Christians' faith being the means by which they entered sacramentally at baptism into a unity with this one seed.[2]

In Romans 4, by contrast, it is specifically the structure of faith which Paul explicates, and in terms of which the relation between Abraham and the Christian believer is established. Decisive for us in connection with Rom. 4 is the fact that the explication of the structure of Abraham's faith as an exposition of Gen. 15 : 6, and its analogy to that of the Christian believer, does not presuppose the reasoning of Gal., but, in fact, constitutes an alternative to the way in which the relationship between the faith of Abraham and the Christian faith was interpreted in the earlier writing. Even more, the reasoning of Gal. is excluded by Rom. 4 : 18–22, where the reference to the promise in the seed of Abraham and his faith in it, is understood to concern specifically Isaac. This hardly makes it possible to maintain the identity of this "one seed" with Christ, as Paul argued in Gal., even if the texts quoted in the two cases may not be altogether identical: Gen. 13 : 5 (cf. 12 : 7; 17 : 7; 22 : 8) in Gal. 3 : 16, and Gen. 15 : 5 in Rom. 4 : 18. What may be Zahn's attempt to overcome this difficulty by emphasizing the lineage of Abraham, Isaac, Jacob and Christ,[3] could only be considered as an attempt to reconcile an apparent conflict between the two passages, without support in the passages themselves.

In Rom. 4, thus, the reasoning is essentially an explication of the structure of faith to which Paul had been brought by 3 : 27–30. In

---

[1] Cf. Jülicher, "Der Brief an die Römer," *Die Schriften des Neuen Testaments neu übersetzt und für die Gegenwart erklärt*, ed. by J. Weiss, vol. II, *Die Briefe. Die johanneische Schriften*, Göttingen: Vandenhoeck und Ruprecht, 1907, pp. 26f.

[2] Cf. above, pp. 80f.

[3] "…the one Christ, the son of Abraham, Isaac and Jacob (Mt. 1 : 1f.) is the universal heir …" *op. cit.*, p. 168; cf. also above, p. 79, footnote 3. Cf. also Michel, *op. cit.* (cf. above, p. 76, footnote 3), p. 127, who, however, fails to take seriously the fact that "the seed" here is Isaac.

contrast with Gal. 3, the interpretation of the significance of Gen.
15 : 6 for the Christian faith here is to the point. The decisive factor
for the relation between Abraham's faith and the faith of the believer, according to this chapter, is the fact that it is the same God
who is the object of the faith of Abraham (4 : 17, cf. 5) and of that
of the Christian believer (verse 24).[1] The connection between them
is established explicitly in verse 23 with the statement that the
justification that was announced to Abraham, was not announced
on his behalf only, "but also on our behalf," i.e., on behalf of Christian believers. God, thus, is not only the identical "object" of the
faith of Abraham and of that of the Christian believer, but also the
identical "subject" of the justification of Abraham and the Christian
believer through faith (4 : 22–24; cf. 4 : 1–8; also 3 : 30).

What is of specific interest for us in the interpretation of Rom. 4,
thus, is the relationship between Abraham and his descendents.
This relationship will be the guiding principle of our interpretation
of the chapter.

1. *Abraham and his Descendents. A Brief Interpretation of Rom. 4*

Rom. 4 : 1 What then shall we say did Abraham our forefather find in
the flesh? (Alternative: 'did Abraham our forefather in the flesh find?').
[2]For if Abraham was justified on the basis of works, he has (reason for)
boasting, but not against God; [3]for what does Scripture say: And Abraham believed God, and it was reckoned to him as righteousness. [4]And to
him who works the pay is not reckoned according to grace but according
to debt: [5]But to him who does not work, believing, however, in him who
justifies the ungodly, his faith is reckoned as righteousness, [6]as even David
pronounces the blessing of the person to whom God reckons righteousness
without works: [7]Blessed of whom the iniquities are forgiven and of whom
the sins are covered. [8]Blessed is the man the sin of whom God does
not reckon. [9]This blessing then, does it apply to the circumcized, or also to
the uncircumcized? For we say: The faith was reckoned to Abraham as
righteousness. [10]How then was it reckoned? When he was in (the state of)
circumcision or in (the state of) uncircumcision: (It was) not in circumcision but in uncircumcision.

[11]And he received (the) sign of circumcision, the seal of the justification

---

1 Cf. Jülicher, *op. cit.*, p. 26; Hans Lietzmann, *An die Römer, Handbuch
zum Neuen Testament*, Tübingen: J. C. B. Mohr (Paul Siebeck), 1933, p. 55;
W. Sanday and A. C. Headlam, *A critical and exegetical Commentary on the
Epistle to the Romans*, Edinburg: T. & T. Clark, reprint of the 5th ed., 1945,
p. 115; Michel, *op. cit.*, p. 127; Leenhardt, *op. cit.*, (cf. above, p. 75, footnote 4),
p. 75; C. K. Barrett, *A Commentary on the Epistle to the Romans*, New York,
Evaston, and London: Harper & Row, 1957, p. 99.

of the faith while in the (state of) uncircumcision, that he should be the father of all who believe through uncircumcision in order that righteous-ness should be reckoned to them, [12] and father of the circumcision for those who are not only from the circumcized, but also follow in the foot-steps of the faith (while) in (the state of) uncircumcision of our father Abraham. [13]For the promise to Abraham or to his seed that he will be the inheritor of the world is not through the Law, but through the righteous-ness of faith. [14]For if those (who are) from the Law are heirs, faith has been emptied, and the promise destroyed .[15]For the Law produces wrath; and where there is no law, (there is) also no transgression. [16]For this reason (it is) from faith, in order that (it be) according to grace, so that the promise be firmly established for every seed, not only for those from the Law, but also for those from the faith of Abraham who is the father of all of us.

[17]—as it is written: I have made you father of many nations—in view of whom he believed, (i.e.) in God who makes alive the dead and calls the none beings as beings. [18]Who against hope in hope believed that he would become father of many nations in accordance with what was said: Thus will your seed be. [19]And without weakening in faith he considered his body which had died, being some hundred years old, and the dead state of the womb of Sarah. [20]In the promise of God he did not doubt through disbelief but he was strengthened through faith, giving glory to God, [21]and convinced that he was capable of also doing what was promised. [22]For that reason it was reckoned to him as righteousness.

[23]And it was not written only on behalf of him that it was reck-oned to him, [24]but also on our behalf to whom it will be reckoned, to those who believe in him who raised Jesus, our Lord from death, [25]he who was delivered up for our transgressions, and was raised for our justification.

a) *The Justification of Abraham* (4 : 1–10)

The question of Rom. 4 : 1, rather than posing a problem, serves as the introduction of Paul's proof-text. He asks: "What did Abra-ham our forefather find?" with the specific intention of answering, not with *charin* as Wilckens insists,[1] but concretely with his proof-text, Gen. 15 : 6. However, before he does so he introduces a direct blow against the justification on the basis of works of the Law, the latter understood in the sense of salvation history. This confirms the general intention of Klein's polemic against a salvation historical interpretation. Wilckens argues that the *kata sarka* in verse 1 gives expression to the physical descent from Abraham,[2] and may be

---

[1] "Die Rechtfertigung Abrahams nach Römer 4," p. 116, cf. also his foot-note 15; again in "Zu Römer 3, 21–4, 25," p. 596, footnote 12; so also Michel, *op. cit.*, p. 115; Leenhardt, *op. cit.*, p. 67.

[2] Cf. "Die Rechtfertigung Abrahams nach Römer 4," p. 122.

correct in doing so, but in precisely that lies the sting of verse 2. "For if Abraham was justified on the basis of works, he has (reason for) boasting," is a concession to the descendants "in the flesh" of Abraham, namely, the recognition that there is a certain justification in works. In 2 : 13b Paul also explicitly affirms a justification of "*doers* of the Law." But, having conceded this in verse 2, he cuts it off from the plan of salvation with "but not before God."[1] This is then substantiated with Gen. 15 : 6.

Wilckens also sees this: "... the exclusive salvation historical privilege of the born Jew as the physical descendent of Abraham is broken by the Christ event."[2] But then he tries to soften his statement by qualifications not derived from the immediate context, but from Rom. 9 : 4f., 11 : 25ff., and 11 : 13ff.[3] Although Paul did express pride in his being "*kata sarka* a Jew," as Wilckens maintains, he explicitly rejected this "as filth in order to gain Christ, and to be found in him, not having my own righteoueness which is out of the Law, but that which is through faith in Christ, the righteousness from God" (Phil. 3 : 8b, 9). And although he did not exclude Jews from salvation, Rom. 4 : 12 makes sufficiently clear that what was determinative for this was the tracing "of the footsteps of the faith while uncircumcised of our father Abraham."

Thus, if Abraham was justified for his works as the Jews claim,[4] he would have reason to boast, but such a boast could not have validity "before God" (verse 2). In verse 3 Paul then substantiates this with his prooftext, Gen. 15 : 6. With the text as such, however, his proof is not yet complete. The Jews also understood Abraham as the example for a life in faith, but faith not in Paul's sense of the

---

[1] So Wilckens, "Die Rechtfertigung Abrahams nach Röm. 4," p. 115; M.-J. Lagrange, *Saint Paul. Épitre aux Romains. Études Bibliques*, Paris: J. Gabalda, 1922, p. 83; Th. Zahn, *Der Brief des Paulus an die Römer*, Leipzig: A. Deichert'sche Verlagsbuchhandlung, 1910, p. 219; Jülicher, *op. cit.*, p. 24; Sanday and Headlam, *op. cit.*, p. 100; also Leenhardt, but with qualification, *op. cit.*, p. 67.

A valid ground for boasting is denied by Paul according to Michel, *op. cit.*, p. 116; C. H. Dodd, *The Epistle of Paul to the Romans. The Moffat New Testament Commentary*, London: Hodder and Stoughton, 1932, references are to the reprint of 1947, p. 68; Barrett, *op. cit.*, p. 87; John Knox, "The Epistle to the Romans," *The Interpreter's Bible*, New York, Nashville: Abingdon Press, vol. IX, 1954, p. 438.

[2] *Op. cit.*, p. 122.

[3] *Op. cit.*, pp. 122f.

[4] Cf Michel, *op. cit.*, p. 115; Leenhardt, *op. cit.*, p. 67; Dodd, *op. cit.*, p. 68.

absence of works. Faith itself was a meritorious act which found further expression in appropriate meritorious acts of faith.[1]

What Paul has to do is to show that Abraham's faith was not a meritorious act, and that contrary to the Jewish understanding, Gen. 15 : 6 was to be interpreted in this sense. He proceeds to do so, first by contrasting as a general principle a reckoning in accordance with what is due on the basis of works and a reckoning in accordance with grace where works are absent, and then, by applying this to the case of Abraham (verses 4f.). Verse 4 is not an exposition of Gen. 15 : 6. It gives expression to a general principle. *elogisthē* = "it was reckoned" in Gen. 15 : 6 by itself does not already establish the absence of works, as is sometimes argued.[2] In verse 4 the same word is used also for what is "reckoned" in accordance with what is due. Paul has to show that the rule of faith without works (3 : 27), i.e., a "reckoning" in accordance with grace, is what applies to Abraham. He states this in verse 4, but his proof that this is correct is not brought until verse 10.

Paul skips one step in his reasoning in verses 4f. After having established that for the person who works the reward is reckoned in accordance with what is due and not in accordance with grace (verse 4), he should logically have continued "to him who does not work (verse 5a) and yet receives something, it is reckoned in accordance with grace." Upon this then, should have followed as the third step: "This is what applies in the case of Abraham." Instead of this, he apparently fused his last two steps,[3] proceeding immediately from step one to the case of Abraham. The phrase "believing in him who justifies the ungodly" apparently applies to Abraham's unmeritorious, precircumcized condition.[4]

Having arrived at the "third" step in this part of his reasoning, Paul's argument is still incomplete. The point to be proved against the Jewish position is precisely that the justification through faith without works applies to the case of Abraham, i.e., that his faith

---

[1] Cf. Billerbeck, *op. cit.*, pp. 184–201, especially p. 188, and specifically with regard to Gen. 15 : 6, pp. 199–201; furthermore, Michel, *op. cit.*, pp. 117f.; Barrett, *op. cit.*, pp. 87f.

[2] So Lagrange, *op. cit.*, p. 86; contra Jülicher, *op. cit.*, p. 24; Knox, *op. cit.*, p. 441; Barrett, *op. cit.*, p. 88.

[3] Cf. Lagrange, *op. cit.*, pp. 86f.; Lietzmann, *op. cit.*, p. 53; Barrett, *op. cit.*, p. 88.

[4] So Leenhardt, *op. cit.*, p. 69; contra Lagrange, *op. cit.*, p. 87; Sanday and Headlam, *op. cit.*, p. 101.

was not a meritorious act and, thus, that his justification was reckoned in accordance with grace. This Paul now does by using another passage of scripture (Ps. 32 : 1f.) to interpret Gen. 15 : 6, not arbitrarily, but on the basis of the rabbinic exegetical rule, *gezerah shewa*, according to which two passages can be used to interpret each other if the same word occurs in both, such as the crucial *"logizein"* = "to reckon" in Paul's two scriptural passages.[1]

But Paul apparently knows that the Jews understood the Psalm passage to apply only to Israel,[2] and so he now in turn uses Gen. 15 : 6 to interpret the Psalm passage (verses 9f.).[3] Psalm 32 : 1f., thus, on the evidence of Gen. 15 : 6 does not apply to Israel only, but to the uncircumcized as well, and specifically to the uncircumcized Abraham. Abraham, thus, was justified through faith without works.

b) *The Problem of Circumcision and the Descendants of Abraham* (4 : 11f.)

Verses 11f. conclude an argument into which Paul had been led already by his quotation of Ps. 32 : 1f., and the fact that this passage was understood by the Jews to apply only to Israel. He formulated the relevant question in a general sense in verse 9a. In this question he does not set up circumcision and non-circumcision as alternatives, but asks whether the blessing of Ps. 32 : 1f. *also* applies to gentiles: "This blessing then, does it apply to the circumcized, or *also* to the uncircumcized?" The added *monon* = "only," after *peritomēn* = "circumcized" in some manuscripts[4] is in agreement with the intention of the text. Paul first applies this to the specific case of Abraham (verses 5b–6) in order to complete his previous argument. In verses 11f. he then takes up the new issue raised by the question of verse 9a and the Jewish understanding of Ps. 32 : 1f.

The fact that Paul mentions those who believe while uncircumcized (verse 11b) first and only then the circumcized (verse 12) as the descendants of Abraham does not establish a principle of pre-

---

[1] Of all the commentaries consulted, the only one which recognized the applicability of this rule was Barrett, *op. cit.*, p. 89.

[2] Cf. Lietzmann, *op. cit.*, p. 53; Michel, *op. cit.*, p. 119.

[3] Cf. Barrett, *op. cit.*, pp. 89f.

[4] Dvg^{ch}

cedence of the uncircumcized.[1] Although the sequence agrees with what happened in the case of Abraham—first faith and then circumcision—its occurrence in our verses is motivated more than anything else by the flow of Paul's argument. He proceeds from the point of view of an assumed advantage of the Jew (cf. the question of verse 9a) and wants to show that in fact Ps. 32 : 1f. also applies to the gentiles. Only when he has done this (verse 11b) does he proceed to add a qualification with regard to the descendants of Abraham from the circumcision as well. Notwithstanding the repetition of *tois* = "to those" in verse 12c: "... to those who follow in the footsteps, etc.," the latter does not refer to a separate group, but is intended as a qualification of "to those who are not only from the circumcision" (verse 12b).[2] In verse 16, incidentally, those who are "from the Law" are mentioned before those who are "from the faith of Abraham."

Paul's reasoning in verses 11f. is based on a certain advantage of the Jew, something which repeatedly comes to the fore all through Romans. So, e.g., even in chapter 2 the advantage of the Jew is the basis of the criticism of him, which leads Paul specifically to ask about this advantage in 3 : 1, affirming it emphatically in 3 : 2a. But, assuming this advantage of the Jew, the problem is: "The gentiles who do not pursue justification, received justification, i.e., the justification by faith, but Israel, pursuing the rule (*nomon*) of righteousness, did not reach the rule. Why?! Because not by faith, but as if by works (did they attempt to achieve righteousness). They stumbled against the rock of stumbling." (9 : 30–32). And so, assuming the advantage of the Jew, and recognizing the problem focused upon by 9 : 30–32, it is understandable that Paul could speak of Israel allegorically as the stem of the cultured olive tree from which the "unbelieving" natural branches were cut out and into which branches of the wild olive tree, i.e., gentiles, were grafted (11 : 17–21).

Thus it would be incorrect to say with Klein that Paul distinguished a double meaning of circumcision in verses 9–12, a soteriological one reserved for Abraham, and an "ethnographic" one, i.e., for the Jews.[3] Paul did distinguish between *real* and *unreal* circum-

---

[1] Contrary to, e.g., Michel, *op. cit.*, p. 120.

[2] This is generally recognized, cf. e.g., Sanday and Headlam, *op. cit.*, p. 108; Lietzmann, *op. cit.*, p. 54; etc.

[3] "Römer 4 und die Idee der Heilsgeschichte," pp. 432f.

cision to such a degree in 2 : 25–29 that someone who was physically circumcized could, by his actions, render his circumcision meaningless, whereas someone who was physically uncircumcized could, again by his actions, realize the true meaning of circumcision.[1] But this is not a distinction between two types of circumcision. Paul's point is that the subjection to the performance of a purely physical circumcision is in fact *not* circumcision, applying the same principle to the being a Jew in a very careful formulation in 2 : 18f., in which he avoided using the terms "Jew" and "circumcision" to what is not a Jew and not circumcision. "Not he who is it in the open, is a Jew, and neither is that which is in the open in the flesh circumcision. But he who is it in concealment is a Jew, and circumcision is of the heart in the spirit, not in the letter." All he did was to distinguish between what is essential and what accidental in his definition of circumcision. One only needs to apply this really very radical principle to Christianity in order to achieve a theology completely out of the ghetto.

However, there may be a difference in the understanding of circumcision in 2 : 25–29 and in our present passage (4 : 9–12) which needs to be taken into consideration, since the former, as part of the section 1 : 18–3 : 20 is subject to the "For all have sinned and fall short of the glory of God" of 3 : 23. Nevertheless, that would not bring about a distinction between the circumcision of Abraham and that of the Jews since Abraham is equally subject to the statement of 3 : 23. By identifying the sign of circumcision of Abraham as a "seal of the justification of (his) faith (while) in the (state of) uncircumcision" (4 : 11),[2] Paul identified the true meaning of circumcision *also* as a Jewish cultic rite.

Thus the reference to Abraham as the "father of the circumcision for those who are not only from the circumcised, but also follow in the footsteps of the faith (while) in (the state of) uncircumcision of our father Abraham" (4 : 12) should be understood in the sense of those who are not only circumcized, i.e., Jews, but also realize the true meaning of their circumcision as the re-presentation of the

---

[1] Cf. Barrett, *op. cit.*, p. 92, in connection with the circumcision of Abraham. "Abraham's circumcision, *rightly understood*, confirms not the doctrine of justification by works of law, but that of justification by faith." (My emphasis).

[2] For a discussion of the question of the meaning of circumcision as a "seal," cf., e.g., Barrett, *op. cit.*, pp. 91f.; Michel, *op. cit.*, pp. 119f.

sign of the faith of Abraham while he was uncircumcized. With that a salvation historical line is broken, because with their circumcision those "who also follow in the footsteps of the faith (while) in (the state of) uncircumcision of our father Abraham" grasp back *cultically* to the event of Abraham's justification by faith.

It is not possible to argue conclusively that circumcision in this sense was not limited to something that could be realized only as an explicit act of faith in Christ, i.e., that its realization was not limited to Jewish *Christians*, but there is nothing in the passage to suggest that Paul's understanding of circumcision was limited in this way.[1] Such an understanding would in any case be contrary to the principle established in 2 : 18f.,[2] irrespective of whether or not Paul would have been willing to apply it here.

Furthermore, the distinctive characteristic of this chapter compared with Gal. 3, namely, its theocentrism compared with the Christocentrism of Gal. 3, should be taken into consideration here. Nowhere in this passage is the faith of Abraham interpreted as explicitly—or for that matter even implicitly—faith in Christ,[3] as was the case in Gal. In any case, it would have been equally impossible for all *Christians* as it would be for non-Christian Jews to follow in the footsteps of the faith of Abraham as understood in Gal., since Abraham's faith relationship to Christ there was understood to have been a unique one, namely, of the expectation of the fulfilment of the promise to *him* in his *one* seed (Gal. 3 : 16). Abraham's faith as interpreted in Gal. was unique to himself.[4]

But in contrast with Gal. where Christ was the determinative factor for the justification by faith, it is the structure of faith as trust in God which is determinative in Rom. The specific form in which, and the occasion on which, this faith came to expression, are apparently indifferent. It is faith "in him who justifies the ungodly" in verse 5; "in God who makes alive the dead and calls what is not into being" in verse 17 with specific reference to the physical condition of Abraham and Sarah in verse 19, and "in him who raised

---

[1] Contra Zahn, *op. cit.*, p. 227, cf. 223ff.; Sanday and Headlam, *op. cit.*, p. 108; Michel, *op. cit.*, p. 120.

[2] Cf. above, p. 90.

[3] Cf. Sanday and Headlam, *op. cit.*, p. 101. "It is rather a departure from St. Paul's more usual practice to make the object of faith God the Father rather than God the Son."

[4] Cf. above, pp. 80f.

Jesus, our Lord from death" in verse 24. This indifference of the specific form and occassion of the faith in God clearly leaves open in principle—and that is what concerns us here—the possibility that Jews who were not Christians could have followed in the footsteps of the faith which Abraham had before he was circumcized.

According to Klein, in 4 : 9–12 Paul "moves beyond the unhistorical category of a paradigm in his interpretation of Abraham,"[1] but points out that the temporal aspect which enters into the picture here is not that of the difference between the time before and the time after the crucifixion of Christ. The temporal aspect in this section concerns Abraham's circumcision and what preceded it.[2] According to rabbinic calculation, too, a period of 29 years transpired between the announcement of the covenant (Gen. 15 : 10) and Abraham's circumcision (Gen. 17 : 10).[3] Important in this is the fact that his justification preceded his circumcision. The historical point, thus, according to Klein, is that it confirms the indifference between circumcision and non-circumcision with regard to the blessing (cf. verse 9).[4]

"Indifference" is probably saying too much, because that would contradict the advantage of the Jew which Paul presupposes all through the letter.[5] But it would be correct to say that the specific historical circumstances of Abraham's justification in relation to his circumcision were decisive for Paul, however, not in order to argue that circumcision or not is indifferent, but to open the way for the entry of the uncircumcized. In the polemical situation of Gal., he did declare circumcision or non-circumcision as indifferent (6 : 15). But there he was arguing from the point of view of the already realized justification by faith in Christ. In Rom. he was more concerned to bring out the true meaning of circumcision as the sign of the faith of Abraham before he was circumcized, in order to establish the faith of Abraham as the only true basis of the argument.

With that Paul did not concede anything as far as the justification by faith is concerned. In Rom. (2 : 25f.) as in Gal. (5 : 3) he understood circumcision as obedience to the Law, and in Rom. (3 : 21) as in Gal. (3 : 25) it was the realization of justification by

---

[1] *Op. cit.*, p. 432.
[2] *Ad loc.*
[3] Cf. Billerbeck, *op. cit.*, vol. III, p. 203; Michel, *op. cit.*, p. 119.
[4] *Ad loc.*
[5] Cf. above, pp. 89f.

faith in Christ which brought to an end the period of the Law. The difference between Gal. and Rom. lies in the fact that in the former Paul was focusing on something that was being required of his converts which he considered to have lost its meaning through the justification in Christ, whereas he focuses on it as a Jewish rite in Rom. with the intention of bringing out its true meaning. Furthermore he may, in the meantime, have been forced to give due recognition to the fact that circumcision did not come 430 years later with the Law (Gal. 3 : 17), and thus, that it was primarily related not to the Law, but to the justification of Abraham. Contrary to Klein, thus, Paul had to face up to the fact that circumcision is not all that indifferent, but still wanted to maintain that it was not necessary for Christians to be circumcized, i.e., that also the physically uncircumcized could be true children of Abraham (4 : 11). This he had done in a preliminary way in 2 : 25–29 by arguing that there is no real difference between the Jew and the gentile as far as physical circumcision is concerned, because the real circumcision is "of the heart, in spirit," and now conclusively in 4 : 9–12 by pointing to the fact that the faith of Abraham preceded his circumcision, thus making circumcision correctly understood, not indifferent, but clearly secondary.

Paul's concern here is less negative, polemical, than Klein suggests. His interest was primarily in the condition of the person on whom the blessing of verses 7f. (Ps. 32 : 1f.) is pronounced, i.e., in the structure of existence of the person who is justified. The historical significance of this with regard to the physical descent of Abraham is secondary. Paul did not argue primarily historically; neither salvation historically nor in Klein's polemical, anti-salvation historical sense. Paul's positive exposition of the structure of existence of the person who is justified by faith, entailed the exclusion of those who do not have faith of the nature of Abraham. This, as a matter of fact, is not even explicitly stated in verses 9–12, but can be inferred from what Paul says positively about those who are the true children of Abraham in verses 11f. This inference Paul now makes explicit in the next section.

c) *Faith and the Law* (4 : 13–16)

In verses 13 – 15 Paul sets up the existence under the Law and the existence in faith as alternatives. "For if those (who are) from the Law are heirs, faith has been emptied and the promise destroyed." (Verse 14). This should not be understood as a purely negative statement about the Law, i.e., in the sense of the Law on the one hand and faith and promise on the other as antagonistic principles. It should rather be understood in the sense of Gal. 3 : 21 where Paul himself poses a similar question: "Is the Law, thus, against the promises?" only to negate it emphatically, adding the explanation: "For if a Law which had the power of giving life was given, justification, in fact, would have been from the Law." The Law, thus, is not against the promises, but could have achieved that which the promises intended if it had been endowed with the power of giving life, making the promises superfluous.

Rom. 4 : 14, thus, should also be understood in this sense of the promise and faith becoming superfluous if justification could have been achieved by the Law (cf. also Rom. 3 : 20–22b). The point is not that a "promise contingent on the fulfilment of a law which no one fulfils in its entirety is a delusion."[1] The inability of man to fulfil the Law is not at issue here, but whether justification is by faith or by the Law, and whether the true descendants of Abraham are those who are under the Law or those who follow in the footsteps of his faith.

Once more it becomes clear that Paul is not specifically anti-Jewish, or against the Law as such, but his exposition of the structure of existence in faith makes it necessary for him to make clear that existence under the Law cannot continue in an existence in faith. This is something he apparently also knew from experience. (Cf. especially, Phil. 3 : 4b–11).

In verse 16 Paul then reaffirms the justification by faith, because only if it is by grace, i.e., through faith in accordance with the promise, and not in accordance with what is due (cf. verse 4) for works done in obedience to a Law, could the promise be assured for all the descendants of Abraham; for those who are under the Law as well as for those who are from faith.[2] In this case Paul distinguishes between two groups only: those who are from the Law and those who are from faith. No intermediary group such as those "who are not only from the circumcized but also follow in the footsteps of the faith ... of Abraham" of verse 12. The reason is obvious: Paul stated too clearly that faith and the Law arc contra

---

[1] Dodd, op. cit., p. 69; so also Lietzmann, op. cit., p. 55; Knox, op. cit., p. 444; better Lagrange, op. cit., pp. 92f.

[2] Cf. Barrett, op. cit., p. 96.

ries (verse 14). Thus he could not speak of "those who are not only from the Law, but also from faith." This shows once more that the situation in connection with the Law and the situation in connection with circumcision are not the same. Faith frees from the Law (Gal. 3 : 25), but, so to speak, fulfils the true meaning of circumcision (Rom. 4 : 11).[1]

Thus, grace, according to our verse, assures the promise also for those who are under the Law, which seems to be an apparent contradiction of verse 4. However, Paul does not say that those who are under the Law will be saved *through obedience to the Law*; only that grace *assures* the promise also for those who are under the Law, i.e., the historical Israel. Quite to the contrary, "in order that (it be) according to grace," it has to be "from faith." (Verse 16b and a). The inclusion of the descendants from the Law under grace, thus expresses, on the one hand, the assurance of the promise also for Israel—notwithstanding her present behaviour (cf. 3 : 3)—and, on the other hand, the hope which Paul still had for those who were under the Law because of the assurance of grace (cf. 10 : 1; 11 : 23,26).[2]

d) *The Faith of Abraham...* (4 : 17–22)

In verse 16 Paul once more focused on the promise to Abraham with the explicit reference to "the promise," and the reference to Abraham "who is the father of all of us" for whom the promise is assured. In order to substantiate that the latter is the sense of the promise to Abraham, he now first quotes Gen. 17 : 5, in verse 17a, and then, in verses 17b–22, reaches back to the beginning of verse 16, to the reference to "faith, in order that (it be) according to grace" as that through which the promise is assured, by tying the promise to Abraham in with his justification through faith in God who gave him the promise. In this way Paul prepared the way to reaffirm (in verses 23–25) the relationship between Abraham and those who believe in Christ, by presenting him as the type for the latter.[3]

---

[1] Cf. above, pp. 89–91.

[2] So Klein, *op. cit.*, pp. 438–440.

[3] For a discussion of typology in the New Testament, cf. Leonhard Goppelt, *Typos. Die typologische Deutung des Alten Testaments im Neuen*, Gütersloh: Gütersloher Verlagshaus Gerd Mohn, 1939, 2nd printing, Darmstadt: Wissenschaftliche Buchgesellschaft, 1966; also "Apokalyptik und Typologie bei Paulus," *Theologische Literaturzeitung*, 89 (1964) cols. 321–344, now also as an appendix to the previously mentioned work, *Typos*, pp. 259–299.

What is most significant in connection with the establishment of Abraham's faith in the promise as the basis of his justification is the fact that, in contrast with Gal. 3 where his faith was in the fulfilment of the promise in his one seed, Christ, his faith in Rom. 4 is understood, much more concretely and immediately, to be concerned with the expected birth of a son by his wife, Sarah, through whom descendants in whom the promise would be fulfilled, were assured. Paul's reasoning in Gal. 3 and that of Rom. 4 should be clearly distinguished. It is altogether incorrect to say that what was stated in Gal. 3 : 6f., is "explicated more precisely and grounded exegetically in Rom. 4."[1] What is stated in Gal. 3 : 6f. is interpreted Christologically in Gal. 3 : 16, cf. verses 26–29. Such a Christology is absent in Rom. 4, and can also not be affirmed on the basis of the reference to Abraham as "inheritor of the world" (Rom. 4 : 13),[2] since this expression is derived not from specifically Christian, but Jewish expectations concerning Abraham.[3]

The "seed" of Abraham was interpreted most inconsistently by Paul *as Christ* in Gal. 3 : 16; which made it possible for him to say that "when you are of Christ, you are seed of Abraham" (verse 29); and *as the physical descendants of Abraham* in Rom. 4 : 18f., with the subsequent qualification "not because they are seed, are all children" (Rom. 9 : 7). With the latter the descendants through Isaac are again excluded from the "children" although they are "seed" of Abraham. Then, however, Paul uses a Scriptural quotation to substantiate this: "in Isaac will your seed be called" (Gen. 21 : 12), with which "the seed" is once more limited to the descendants of Isaac. In verse 8 he underscores this limitation with the statement that "the children of the promise are the *seed*." A further limitation of the childhood of Abraham is made in verses 10–13 with the exclusion of Esau.

e) *...the type of Christian faith.* (4 : 23–25)

Nevertheless already in Rom. 4 : 17ff., Paul probably had in mind what now becomes explicit in verses 23–25, namely, that "the

---

[1] Goppelt, *Typos*, p. 164, cf. 165. A similar confusion occurs in Barrett, *From first Adam to Last*, pp. 41f.
[2] Contra Michel, *op. cit.*, p. 121; cf. also Jülicher, *op. cit.*, p. 25.
[3] Cf. Billerbeck, *op. cit.*, p. 209 (with quotations), although, as Lietzmann, *op. cit.*, p. 54, points out, of the quotations given by Billerbeck, only *Mechilta Ex. 14 : 31* does not originate in the late Middle Ages. So also Lagrange, *op. cit.*, p. 92, cf. also Barrett, *op. cit.*, p. 94.

faith of Abraham rejoins ours, since, as we know, the end of the promise is Christ."[1] His real concern is the justification by faith without works as realized by those who believe in Christ. And so, in these verses, he comes out at a Christologically grounded faith. However, that does not diminish the difference between Gal. 3 and Rom. 4 as far as the Christology is concerned. Whereas Christology is explicit and in the center in the former, it is at the most a "functional" Christology of sorts in Rom. 4, with God and the believer's relationship to him, i.e., of Abraham and of the Christian, in the center. In this case the relationship between Abraham and the Christian believer is not Christologically determined, as had been the case in Gal. 3. In our passage the relationship between them is understood in the sense of the justification of Abraham through faith being the type for the Christian believers' justification through faith in God who raised Jesus from the dead (verses 23f.).[2] This typology is absent in Gal. 3 where the same function was performed by the Christology (verses 16 and 26–39).[3]

The analogy between Abraham's faith and that of the Christian believer in Rom. 4 is strengthened by the fact that both believe in God, who "makes alive the dead" (verse 17, cf. 24).[4] An explicit Christology in introduced by Paul only at the end of the chapter (verse 25), but not as part of the actual reasoning. It merely rounds off the statement concerning the justification of the believer through his faith in God who raised Jesus from the dead, but nevertheless, was probably of decisive meaning for Paul as a confirmation of the Christological foundation of faith.[5]

It could hardly be anything else than a misunderstanding of what Paul intended which led Dodd, followed by Knox, to conclude that Paul applied the "fine definition of faith" which he deduced "with a somewhat artificial treatment of Scripture," "not without a trace of the same artificiality, to the faith of a Christian."[6] A misunderstanding must result if one assumes, as Knox does, that the connection is determined by what was *accomplished* in the acts of God.

---

[1] Lagrange, *op. cit.*, p. 97.

[2] Cf., in particular, Goppelt, *Typos*, pp. 165f.

[3] Contra Goppelt, *ad loc.*

[4] Cf. Jülicher, *op. cit.*, p. 26; Lietzmann, *op. cit.*, p. 55; Sanday and Headlam, *op. cit.*, p. 113; Leenhardt, *op. cit.*, p. 75; Barrett, *The Epistle to the Romans*, p. 99.

[5] Cf. Jülicher, *op. cit.*, p. 27.

[6] Dodd, *op. cit.*, p. 70; cf. Knox, *op. cit.*, p. 448.

"Such a description (i.e., of Abraham's faith in Rom. 4 : 17) is intended to remind the reader not only of Isaac's birth ..., but also of Christ's resurrection from the dead—as well as perhaps, the new life found within the Christian community."[1] Here Paul's reasoning is allegorized where he did not intend allegory. The connection for Paul existed in the identity of God who acted, and the structure of existence in faith of Abraham and the Christian believer. The analogy of the acts in verses 17–19 and 24 only serves to underscore the identity of God who acted, and the analogy of the faith of Abraham and the Christian believer. If there is a problem here, it is not the application of the definition of faith deduced from the case of Abraham to the faith of the Christian believer, but the fact that faith is here understood un-Christologically, making the interpretation in terms of a typology possible.

2. *What is at issue in Rom. 4*

A fundamental issue in connection with this passage—for us *the* fundamental issue—was recognized by both Wilckens and Klein, but already with all the desired clarity by Jülicher.[2] Wilckens argues that if it is not history, but the structure of faith that is important here, then one must take into consideration "a fundamental disposability of the Old Testament for the Christian faith;" then it is not clear "why Paul could not have taken recourse to extra Old Testament examples for Christian justification faith ('Rechtfertigungsglauben') instead of Abraham."[3] "To be a Christian would then not be essentially, i.e., not in the sense of the history of salvation, filiation of Abraham, and the Church not essentially Israel."[4]

Klein correctly objects against this unfounded identification of "essential" and "salvation historical."[5] That this identification is not necessary is also shown by the sense in which Lietzmann uses the term "essence, essential," when he states that in verses 17–24 Paul finds an "essential relationship" in the *content* of Abraham's faith and that of the believer. This essential relationship consists in the fact that it was God's power to resurrect the dead that was to be

---

[1] Knox, *op. cit.*, p. 446.
[2] *Op. cit.*, pp. 26f.; cf. below, p. 100.
[3] "Die Rechtfertigung Abrahams nach Römer 4," p. 114.
[4] *Ad loc.*
[5] "Römer 4 und die Idee der Heilsgeschichte," pp. 442f.

believed: Thus Abraham believed (verse 19), and thus we too believe (verse 24).[1] Here the essential relationship is understood precisely structurally and not salvation historically.

Nevertheless, Klein's valid objection against Wilcken's identification of "essential" and "salvation historical" does not eliminate the problem recognized by the latter. What Wilckens is really concerned about is that if the relationship between Abraham and the Christian believer is limited to the structural analogy of their faith, there would be no basis for a unique relationship of the Christian believer to Abraham as his "father." His question is: Why could Paul not have taken recourse to extra Old Testament examples for Christian faith, instead of Abraham?[2]

Klein is also convinced that Abraham was not understood by Paul as a "symbol for a truth which could in principle be exchanged at will (for another). In such a case (this truth) must of necessity become general."[3] He understands the problem in Romans to be how Abraham, who lived in the time before the righteousness of God in Christ could have been experienced, could be presented as the Scriptural proof for the righteousness of God.[4] With that Wilckens' question was substituted by a more fundamental one, namely, why in the first place Paul took recourse to Abraham as the example for the Christian faith. Could he validly serve the purpose of such an example? Does that not mean, according to Klein, that "the event of justification should of necessity be freed from its historical reference to become a general truth?"[5] He is convinced that Paul did not understand justification in this sense. "There is a continuity from Abraham as an historical figure to the present faith, but it is not the product of an historical development, and in no way demonstrable. Rather, this continuity *arises* for the first time where one believes as Abraham did. The continuity between Abraham and the believer, thus, is a projection back ('ein Rückentwurf') of contemporary faith, as such imperceptable and itself entirely an object of faith."[6] "Abraham *is* no one's father,—he *becomes* the father in and through faith."[7]

---

[1] *Op. cit.*, p. 55.
[2] Wilckens, *ad loc.*
[3] *Op. cit.*, p. 431.
[4] *Op. cit.*, p. 429, cf. above, pp. 76f.
[5] *Ad loc.*
[6] *Op. cit.*, p. 435.
[7] *Op. cit.*, p. 436.

With that Klein's understanding of faith does not escape a certain arbitrariness. What he would have to answer is why contemporary faith cannot project back a continuity between other individuals and the believer. Is the inexchangeability of Abraham not an act "at will," to use one of his own expressions?[1] The author of Hebrews (cf. 11 : 1–12 : 1) and Karl Barth,[2] in any case, did not limit the projection back of Christian faith in this way; Barth including even Socrates and the Platonic philosophy with his examples.[3]

Jülicher went one step further in explaining why Paul took recourse to Abraham as the example for Christian faith. He formulated the problem of Rom. 4 with all the desirable accuracy as follows. "Since Abraham's faith could not have this content (i.e., of Rom. 4 : 24), directed as it was to quite a different promise, the question arises: Can his justification be regarded as the same as ours which follows from faith in Jesus (3 : 26)? And if it could (be regarded as such), is a justification without Christ's atoning work then not also possible? Has (such a justification) then not been shown to have been real long before (Christ)? And if not, what is the sense then of the Scriptural proof?"[4] Jülicher is almost certainly correct when he states that Paul would probably have found an escape in the direction of Gal. 3 : 16 if he had been confronted with these questions,[5] although he could not have taken recourse to quite the reasoning of Gal. 3 : 16 without once more contradicting the discussion in Rom. 4 : 17–22.

The reason why Paul could take recourse to Abraham as the example for Christian faith is then identified as follows by Jülicher. "He did not perceive the piercing here by himself (similarly in 2 : 14f.) of his system, which permits no righteousness, only sin and wrath, to people before Christ. The inconsistency can be explained, in view of the exclusiveness of the contraries 'works and faith,' by the fact that in his thinking, just as no other works come into consideration but those that are of the Law, so also no other faith than

---

[1] *Op. cit.*, p. 431; cf. above, p. 99.

[2] *Der Römerbrief*, Zollikon–Zürich: Evangelischer Verlag, 8th printing of the 2nd ed., 1947, p. 93, cf. 118; Eng. tr. by Edwyn C. Hoskyns, *The Epistle to the Romans*, London, New York, Toronto: Oxford University Press, 1933, p. 117, cf. 141.

[3] *Op. cit.*, pp. 93 and 118, respectively; Eng. tr., pp. 117 and 141.

[4] *Op. cit.*, p. 26.

[5] *Ad loc.*

that which is in Jesus Christ, our Lord. He lives so completely in his present and reviews everything in history so onesidedly only from the point of view given by the present, that he immediately greets as a witness for *his* faith wherever there is talk about faith in the Bible."[1]

No further argument is necessary to show that a similar understanding led the author of Hebrews and Barth to believe that the faith of their examples found their fulfillment in the faith in Christ.

The "piercing by (Paul) himself of his system"[2] is not appreciated by Jülicher, who maintains "that Paul does not allow himself to be led astray to obscure his gospel (i.e.), he does not let the new comply with the old in order to increase the argument drawn from the old."[3] For this Rom. 4 : 24f. alone, with which our passage is concluded, is proof enough,[4] since here faith is once more identified as faith in Christ.

Significant for a theology out of the ghetto is the fact, recognized but not appreciated by Jülicher, that Paul himself pierced his own system of thought in Rom. 4, even if he probably did not intend to do so, as Jülicher also saw. Paul almost certainly would not have conceded an analogy between the faith of Abraham and the faith in Christ if he had to concede at the same time that the former had nothing specifically to do with Christ. Although Rom. 4 : 17–22 contradicts the reasoning of Gal. 3 : 16, Paul almost certainly had not given up what he had tried to prove with the latter text.

Nevertheless, in Rom. 4, he did establish an analogy between the faith of Abraham and that of the Christian believer; an analogy which was not dependent on the reference to Christ since this reference applies only in the case of the faith of the latter, contrary to Gal. 3 : 16. The reason for this is that Paul had let himself in on a philosophical problem, namely, that of definition, and performed so well that he pierced his own system. Very much like Socrates who asked, e.g: What is bravery? in the *Laches*, or: What is virtue? in the *Meno*, Paul in Rom. 4, asked: What is faith through which one is justified? And he had been led to this problem by a consideration

---

[1] *Op. cit.*, pp. 26f.
[2] Jülicher, *op. cit.*, p. 26; cf. above, p. 100.
[3] *Op. cit.*, p. 27.
[4] *Ad loc.*

very similar to that which prompted Socrates' inquiries,[1] namely, how is it that Scripture says about Abraham that he "believed God and it was reckoned to him as justification" (Gen. 15 : 6, cf. Rom. 4 : 3 and Gal. 3 : 6), and we say that the Christian believer is justified through faith in Christ (Rom. 3 : 22, cf. 26, 28)? The answer to this question is to be found in the answer to the question what faith is through which the believer is justified. As a matter of fact, Paul had already taken two trial runs in the practice of definition, although of a slightly different nature, in 2 : 12–16: What is justification by the Law? and 2 : 25–29: What is circumcision or being a Jew?

Unlike Socrates, Paul's inquiries did not end inconclusively. He was also not interested in the philosophical question as such. Nevertheless, in Rom. 4 he did not impose the Christian concept of faith on Abraham, as the author of Hebrews and Barth did, and as he himself did even more explicitly in Gal. 3 : 16. In Rom. 4, with remarkable keenness, he tried to discover what it was that transcended the two instances of justification through faith with which he was concerned, i.e., what the essence of justification through faith was. In doing so he could not prevent the reference to Christ in the justification of the believer from becoming an accidental in the definition of the justification through faith. It is true that he may not have been quite ready for this result of his own reasoning, but Rom. 2 : 12–16 and 25–29 reveal that this kind of reasoning was not altogether incidental with Paul. And if it carried weight in his anti-Jewish polemics, it ought to carry weight when it pierces his own system of thought.

In any case, it is clear that in Paul's mind there was a level of thought that was not caught up within the framework of what Jülicher calls his "system," i.e., thinking that was bound by the reference to Christ as its center. In Rom. 4 the justification of Abraham formed another center. Moreover, Rom. 2 : 12–16 and 25–29 reveal that this level of thought was methodologically independent and could be applied equally well in relation to Judaistic and to Christian thinking.

In Rom. 4, thus, Paul showed a way for a theology out of the

---

[1] For a readily accessible introduction to the Socratic problem, cf. Gottfried Martin, *Einleitung in die allgemeine Metaphysik*, Köln: Kölner Universitätsverlag, 1957; Eng. tr. by Eva Schaper and Ivor Leclerc, *An Introduction to General Metaphysics*, London: George Allen and Unwin Ltd., 1961.

ghetto. With verse 25 he may have tried to block it again, but only intuitively, since he probably did not even perceive what he had done, as Jülicher points out.[1] However, in fact he did not block the way, but simply did not proceed on it. He almost certainly was not even aware that this escape was there. If he had been confronted with this fact, he might very well have tried to block it by arguing in a way similar to Gal. 3 : 16, as Jülicher maintains.[2] But that could hardly be convincing. It could be better to surrender Abraham's justification as the type of the Christian's justification through faith, because that is where the problem lies. Abraham's faith was not the type of the Christian faith in the sense of what Jülicher calls Paul's "system."

But that does not take away from the fact that in Rom. 4 Paul was willing to take note of Abraham outside of his own Christological framework. In Gal. 3 he did not care to take note of the Genesis account of the justification of Abraham, but made use of it in the sense of a monologue, interpreting it as it suited him. In Rom. 4, however, he let himself in on a dialogue with the Genesis account to such an extent that he allowed a continuity between Abraham and the Christian believer which was not dependent on the reference to Christ to become evident. The latter reference qualified only the Christian's faith. No subsequent return to a monologue can nullify the fact that in Rom. 4 a genuine dialogue had taken place between the Christian Paul and the non-Christian Genesis account of the justification of Abraham. It is true, of course, that Paul was not aware that the Genesis account was non-Christian. It was a fundamental assumption for him that it was Christian. That is also the reason why it played such an important part in Gal. 3 as well as in Rom. 4. But it is equally true that Genesis is non-Christian, and in Rom. 4 Paul's erroneous assumption about Genesis never interfered with his argument. In this way unintentionally he allowed the Genesis account in on the argument in its true character as a non-Christian account. It is this allowing the Genesis account to be its true self in his reasoning—unintentionally, but, nevertheless effectively—which makes Rom. 4 a geniune dialogue with the non-Christian world.

In effect, thus, Paul recognized the non-Christian character of the

[1] *Op. cit.*, p. 26; cf. above, pp. 100f.
[2] *Ad loc.*; cf. above, p. 100.

Genesis account, and in this way temporarily stepped out of his ghetto. This may come as a warning to Christians who are willing to engage in dialogue with the world, and each other, without a clear understanding of the identity of the partner admitted to the dialogue. Paul's erroneous assumption about the supposedly Christian Genesis account did not prevent it from asserting itself in its true non-Christian character in the argument of Rom. 4.[1]

---

[1] The following two works, which have particular significance for this problem, appeared after the completion of the present study. Käsemann, "Der Glaube Abrahams in Röm. 4," *Paulinische Perspektive*, Tübingen: J. C. B. Mohr (Paul Siebeck), 1969, pp. 140–177; and Ulrich Luz, *Das Geschichtsverständnis des Paulus*, München: Chr. Kaiser Verlag, 1968, particularly pp. 168–186. Since neither of these works lead me to believe that anything essential needs to be changed in my interpretation, I have not incorporated them into the discussion.

CONCLUSION

It has not been the intention of this study to deny that it is characteristic of the New Testament proclamation to claim that an authentic existence cannot be realized except in response to the proclamation of Christ. What it did intend to show was that within the New Testament there were instances where this claim of exclusiveness is either not recognized—in the ministry of Jesus—, or broken—in the description of the last judgment (Mt. 25 : 31-46) and in Paul's presentation of Abraham as the type of the Christian believer in Rom. 4.

Each of these has a different relationship towards the ghetto of religious exclusiveness: Jesus stood outside of such a ghetto and in his ministry justified such a stance as the fulfilment of what was expected by the pious in their religious exclusiveness; in the description of the last judgment the true meaning of the confession of Christ was interpreted from within the framework of a Christian confessional exclusiveness with non-Christian acts, thus breaking the confessional framework; and in Rom. 4 Paul allowed himself to get involved in the non-Christian Genesis account of the justification of Abraham to such a degree that he could not prevent the reference to Christ from becoming an accidental in the definition of justification through faith, i.e., ceasing to be an essential feature of faith.

Characteristic of all three of these is the recognition of the fellowman. This may be the least apparent in the case of Rom. 4 since it was Abraham's justification through faith in God on which Paul focused in this chapter. God figures very centrally in his presentation. And that is the point. In religious exclusiveness a captive God functions to isolate the believer from his fellowman as fellow man. In all three of our instances a freed God functioned to open the way to the recognition of the fellow man. In Gal. Paul missed Abraham because he had eyes only for his own God, kept in bonds by the confession of Christ. By denying the fellowman's God, the fellowman is ignored. But in Romans, God was freed for the sake of the fellowman Abraham, leading in effect to the recognition of Abraham for what he was, a non-Christian.

God, it appears, is a cypher for the range of one's vision. The present study was concerned with the opening of this vision for the fellowman. But also the fellowman can serve to keep God within bounds, thus limiting the range of vision only to that which has some human value. Our very language is evidence of this. The opening of the range of one's vision does not have to stop with the fellowman, but can also free man for the world. The question of a theology out of the ghetto, thus, is a question of how big one's God is; or how wide the range of one's vision is; or, finally, what is encompassed in one's world.

APPENDIX

THE RECENT HISTORY OF THE INTERPRETATION
OF THE PARABLE CHAPTER, MARK 4

A. The History of the Interpretation of Mk. 4 : 11

The history of the interpretation of this verse is involved. Only the main points will be singled out here. Adolf Jülicher[1] already formulated the situation clearly. "To the masses the parables are given in order that they may have something for the eyes and the ears—: They should remain what they are; should by no means turn around on the way to forgiveness."[2] "To those outside the totality of what Jesus says—comes *en parabolais*, and that does not mean: In parables without an added interpretation, but (simply): In parables. To the (disciples) it is not given in this way. That which is a secret concerning the Kingdom of God for all others, has already been given to them."[3] Thus, he could also say that "according to Mark's theory, speaking in parables would never have been used if there had been only 'disciples,' in which case there would also not have been a need for *epilysis*."[4] The only reason why the solutions were given was because the disciples who heard everything Jesus said, were also addressed in the parables, as they could not have stood around fruitlessly, but could not understand them without a solution.[5] Jülicher believed that verses 11f. were part of Mark's own parable theory which was an attempt to give a satisfactory explanation for the failure of the majority of Israel to respond to the teaching of Jesus.[6]

William Wrede[7] agrees with almost everything Jülicher said about this verse.[8] He left no doubt, however, that this conception of the parables made no sense whatsoever: "For to make incomprehensible

---

[1] *Die Gleichnisreden Jesu*, cf. above, p. 11, footnote 1.
[2] *Op. cit.*, p. 122.
[3] *Op. cit.*, p. 124.
[4] *Ad loc.*
[5] *Ad loc.*
[6] *Op. cit.*, p. 135.
[7] *Das Messiasgeheimnis in den Evangelien*, cf. above, p. 11, footnote 4.
[8] Cf. pp. 54–65.

speeches for the purpose of making others stubborn is horrible. To expect this of speeches—and particularly of parables!—is (more than remarkable), and to want to produce an unreceptivity which in reality is already there is senseless."[1] Wrede, thus, regarded verses 11f. as an expression of the "total conception" of Mark, which, according to him, was the theory of the Messianic secret.[2]

The form and language of our verse convinced Joachim Jeremias[3] that it was of Palestinian origin;[4] thus, he assumes, without any additional evidence, that it is an authentic saying of Jesus.[5] He attaches considerable weight to the apparent antithetical parallelism in the verse, arguing that the words *mystērion* and *parabolē* must co-ordinate antithetically. This would not be the case if *parabolē* here means a parable, but would be true if it translates an original Hebrew *mashal* or Aramaic *mathla*, which means a riddle. Only then does one have an exact antithesis: To you the secret is revealed—those outside are faced with riddles. A material parallel occurs in John 15 : 25, "An hour comes when I will no longer speak in obscure sayings (*paroimia*) to you, but openly (*parrēsia*)...."[6]

It should be noted, however, that Jeremias does not understand this in the sense of those outside being confronted with riddles by Jesus, but that what Jesus taught *remained* riddles *to them*. So, e.g., in the statement: "... for those outside the words of Jesus remain obscure, because they do not recognize his mission, nor do they do penance."[7] He substantiated this interpretation in two ways. In the earlier editions he argued that in our verse *ginesthai en* does not mean the usual "to occur in," but describes a condition in which a person or thing finds him- or itself, in which case it is really a substitute for *einai en* when used in cases such as *einai en barei* "to be demanding" (I Thess. 2 : 7). Some examples of this usage are *ginesthai en ekstasei* "to be ecstatic" (Acts 22 : 17) and *ginesthai en epithymiai tinos* "to be desirous of someone" (Susanna 8 Theod.).

However, all the examples of the usage of *ginesthai en* to which

---

[1] *Op. cit.*, p. 61.
[2] *Op. cit.*, pp. 58–64.
[3] *Die Gleichnisse Jesu*, cf. above, p. 11, footnote 1.
[4] *Op. cit.*, pp. (8f.), 11f.; Eng. tr., p. 15.
[5] *Op. cit.*, pp. (11f.), 14; Eng. tr., p. 18.
[6] *Op. cit.*, pp. (10), 12; Eng. tr., p. 16 in which, however, the reference to John 16 : 25 is missing.
[7] *Op. cit.*, pp. (11), 14; Eng. tr., p. 18.

Jeremias refers concern conditions into which persons have come to be and not conditions in which they simply were. So, e.g., in the case of Susanna 8 *ginesthai en* is used when the elders had come to be in their state of desirousness, thus, "they *had come to be desirous* of her," but in verse 20 where this was an already existing condition, they say to Susanna, *en epithumiai soy esmen* = "we *are* desirous of you." Thus, if *ginesthai en* was used in this sense in our verse, it would have meant "to those outside everything has *come to be* obscure," in which case one has to assume that the preaching of Jesus functioned to bring about a condition of obscurity where it did not previously exist, or that his preaching which was previously clear "has come to be obscure to those outside." Neither of these possibilities appears to be probable.

Günther Bornkamm formulated the decisive criticism against Jeremias' reasoning. "Both halves of the verse speak of something that is imparted."[1] His further criticism, however, that "the sense of *parabolai* is already determined by Mk. 4 : 10 and could only mean the teaching form of the parable"[2] does not affect Jeremias' reasoning, as Jeremias correctly regards the present context as secondary.[3] Nevertheless, Bornkamm's suggestion that the word in our verse was understood "as a speaking in riddles ('Rätselrede') in accordance with a meaning of 'mashal' which was also current"[4] is almost certainly correct.

Without indicating why, Jeremias altered his reasoning in the 6th edition of *Die Gleichnisse Jesu*. This, however, did not prevent him from still coming out at the earlier point. He now indicated that the verse does state that to those outside "everything is imparted in riddles ('rätselhafter Rede'),"[5] but only to interpret this as meaning "to them everything remains obscure," which is his original point. What he in fact wants to maintain is that the reason why the teaching of Jesus as a whole, and not only in the parables, was in riddles to those outside was not because Jesus did not intend them to

---

[1] *Jesus von Nazareth*, Urban Wissenschaftliche Taschenbuch 19, p. 183, note 11; Eng. tr. by Irene and Fraser McLuskey with James M. Robinson, *Jesus of Nazareth*, New York: Harper & Brothers, 1960, p. 201, footnote 11.

[2] *Ad loc.*

[3] *Op. cit.*, pp. (8), 10; Eng. tr., p. 14.

[4] *Ad loc.*

[5] *Op. cit.*, p. 13; Eng. tr., p. 16, incidently using both of Bornkamm's terms.

understand, but because they were *unwilling* to recognize his mission.[1]

If Jeremias was successful in this, it would be no mean theological feat because he would then also be able to maintain that the preaching of Jesus could not have been understood unless his mission was recognized, which would already be a rather explicit Christology. We see almost the Johannine Christ emerge here. Cf., e.g., the Johannine statement: "For he whom the Father has sent, speaks the words of God" (3 : 34, cf. 5 : 36–38, 6 : 29, and frequently elsewhere).

This interpretation finds further support in Jeremias' understanding of verse 12, which will be discussed in the next section.[2] So he can finally say that the saying describes the destiny of all proclamation of the gospel, which is always at the same time the offer of grace and the disaster of condemnation; salvation and offense; redemption and ruin; life and death. It was Mark who introduced the saying into the parable chapter, misled by the translation of *dilᵉma* with *parabolē* which he misunderstood in the sense of "parable," and thus the saying as a reference specifically to the parables. The saying probably originated in the time of the esoteric preaching of Jesus after the confession of Peter when the sharp contrast between the disciples and those "who are outside" is best understandable.[3]

James M. Robinson[4] argued for an interpretation very much like that to which Jeremias ultimately came, without, however, the almost explicit Johannine type of Christology. He took up Jeremias' reasoning about Is. 6 : 9f. positively.[5] In line with the Targum and the rabbinic exegesis, according to Robinson, Mark understood Is. 6 : 10 (cf. Mk. 10 : 12b) as an expression of God's promise in the face of the stubbornness of the people. "Such an interpretation agrees with the divine 'gift' of Mk. 4 : 11, and brings the statement of verse 12a in the full sense of the cosmic struggle in sharp contrast with the activity of God."[6] Thus, he states explicitly that the stub-

---

[1] Cf. *op. cit.*, pp. (11), 14; Eng. tr., p. 18.

[2] Cf. below, Appendix B.

[3] *Op. cit.*, pp. (11f.), 14; Eng. tr., p. 18.

[4] *Das Geschichtsverständnis des Markus-Evangeliums*, cf. above, p. 11, footnote 1, cf. also *The Problem of History in Mark*, Naperville: Alec R. Allenson, Inc., 1957 (abbreviated *Problem* below).

[5] Cf. below, Appendix B, for Jeremias' interpretation.

[6] *Geschichtsverständnis*, p. 72, footnote 33.

bornness and lack of understanding of the disciples, referred to in 8 : 17, 21, "was already anticipated by 4 : 13 where the disciples, fully like those outside, do not understand the parable."[1] Wrede also recognized that what is said about the crowds in 4 : 12, is subsequently, in 8 : 17f., also said about the disciples.[2]

According to Robinson, in Mark's gospel Jesus' proclamation of the Kingdom of God (1 : 15) is the divine gift, i.e., the "secret of the Kingdom" (4 : 11), and this gift of the new truth creates a new situation, i.e., of liberation ("conversion" 1 : 15).[3] But correct understanding itself is possible only as a gift of God,[4] and "although the disciples 'had been given' the secret of the Kingdom of God (4 : 11, 34), they continue to need the admonition to listen, as the parable of the sower shows ...."[5] Here, then, the distinction between the disciples and those outside is interpreted as being, not ontological, but ontic, i.e., not a normal condition but one that was brought about by the response to the proclamation of Jesus. This is not contradicted by Robinson's suggestion that "Mk. 4 : 10–25 may also be the reflection of Mark's awareness of the rejection of the Jews ..., (and) may reasonably be associated with the theological problem posed by the general failure of the Jewish mission."[6] The latter view, however, for which Robinson refers to Lightfoot, but which had been suggested previously by D. F. Strauss and H. C. Holtzmann, was already rejected by Wrede.[7]

An interpretation of Mk. 4 : 11f. which follows Jeremias very closely, and yet differs from him in one very significant point, was suggested by Willi Marxsen.[8] A comparison of the structure of Mk. 4 : 1–10, 13–20 with that of 7 : 14–23 convinced him that this structure (viz., the presentation of the parable followed by an interpretation, in a consistent form) was already characteristic of a layer of tradition preceding the miracle source in which Mark encountered the parable of the sower and its interpretation. Between the parable

---

[1] *Geschichtsverständnis*, p. 70.
[2] Cf. *op. cit.*, p. 64, footnote 1.
[3] *Geschichtsverständnis*, p. 72.
[4] *Geschichtsverständnis*, p. 102, cf. *Problem*, p. 50.
[5] *Geschichtsverständnis*, p. 70; cf. also his discussion of the two levels of understanding, which he regards as the theme of Mk. 4, in *Problem*, p. 77.
[6] *Problem*, p. 66, footnote 2; also *Geschichtsverständnis*, p. 99, footnote 22.
[7] Cf. *op. cit.*, p. 64, footnote 2.
[8] "Redaktionsgeschichtliche Erklärung der sogenannten Parabeltheorie des Markus," *Zeitschrift für Theologie und Kirche*, 52 (1955), pp. 255–271.

of the sower (4 : 1–10), which he considered a *mashal*, and its interpretation (verses 13–20), Mark added a second *mashal* (verses 11f.) as an interpretation of the first.[1] For this type of procedure Marxsen refers to the practice in apocalypticism to interpret an obscure *mashal* with a second revelation speech which is itself a *mashal*.[2]

Thus, he agrees with Jeremias that *parabolē* in Mk. 4 : 11f. means *mashal*, but contrary to him maintains that Mark was aware of this, and intended the saying to be understood in this sense.[3] Mark, however, did not formulate the saying himself, but took it over from his tradition. This is indicated by the greater degree of agreement between Mt. 13 : 11, 14 and Lk. 8 : 10, compared with Mk. 4 : 11f.[4]

Marxsen, thus, takes Mk. 4 : 11f. as a saying which Mark took over from his tradition and adapted as an interpretation of the parable of the sower. The saying and the parable were interpreted by Mark from his own situation, i.e., the situation of the church for whom the interpretation was needed. This application to the situation of the church was achieved by extending the group to which the interpretation was given in the double reference to the hearers in verse 10. This would be true irrespective of which of the references to the hearers in this verse came from the source and which from Mark himself. The interpretation no longer applied only to the disciples. It now included the church as well.[5] A similar objective was pursued in the alteration of what was originally a singular in the same verse (a question about the parable of the sower) to a plural (a question about all the parables). The proclamation in this one parable thus became a paradigm for the proclamation as a whole, and, whatever the saying of verse 11f. meant originally, in the Markan context it was understood to refer to what happened to the proclamation in the church at the time of the evangelist.[6]

Thus, according to Mark's gospel, what is sown (by the sower) is the proclamation, which has as its content the mystery of the Kingdom, i.e., Jesus as the Messiah. When this proclamation falls on the way, the rocks, and among the thorns (according to verses 11f. "to those outside"), it bears no fruit, but when it falls on good soil, the

---

[1] *Op. cit.*, pp. 266f.
[2] *Op. cit.*, p. 266.
[3] *Op. cit.*, p. 264.
[4] *Ad loc.*, footnote 1; cf. below, Appendix C.
[5] *Op. cit.*, pp. 266f.
[6] *Op. cit.*, p. 267.

harvest is great.[1] The church has recognized the Messiah in Jesus because those inside "have the 'interpretation' by the Father, who 'gives' this *mystērion*, (and thus) one has access, through the spirit, to the *mystērion*."[2] And so, ultimately, Marxsen comes to an interpretation of Mk. 4 : 11f. very similar to that of Jeremias, except for one important difference. "To those outside everything comes *en parabolais*, (i.e.,) for them everything remains obscure. They can hear the proclamation and yet they do not hear it. The same seed is sown, (but) the result of the sowing is very different."[3] Also in the interpretation of verse 12 Marxsen follows Jeremias very closely.[4] The difference between Marxsen and Jeremias lies in the fact that what Jeremias regards as an authentic saying of Jesus giving expression to the actual situation of his ministry, but which was misunderstood by Mark, is considered by Marxsen in its present context as an expression of Markan theology, reflecting the situation of the church in his own time.

Equally unacceptable in Marxsen's interpretation, as it is in that of Jeremias, is the fact that he understands *en parabolais* in verse 11 as referring at the same time to the parables as part of the proclamation (even though as *mᵉshalim* they are in need of interpretation), and to the obscurity in which everything remains for those outside.[5] The only possible reconciliation of these meanings would seem to be if verse 11 meant "to those outside everything came in parables *without interpretation*," but as Jülicher[6] has shown, this is not what the verse says. The verse simply states that it came to them "in parables," without qualification. Thus, only one of the meanings of *en parabolais*, required by the interpretations of Jeremias and Marxsen, is possible; and since the reference to the proclamation which is intended for all is excluded by the contrast between "those around him with the twelve" and "those outside," *en parabolais* can refer only to what is intended specifically for those outside, which leaves them without understanding, as the next verse indicates.

The objection against the interpretations of Jeremias and Marxsen—and this affects the interpretation of Robinson as well—is

---

[1] *Op. cit.*, p. 268.

[2] *Ad loc.*

[3] *Op. cit.*, pp. 268f.

[4] Cf. below, Appendix B.

[5] Cf. Jeremias, *op. cit.*, pp. 13f.; Eng. tr., pp. 16–18; Marxsen, *op. cit.*, pp. 268f.

[6] *Op. cit.*, p. 124.

strengthened by the fact that their understanding of the saying, as a reference to what happens to the proclamation, prevents them from accepting that the intention of the parables according to the saying of Mk. 4 : 11 is to keep those outside from understanding. This comes out clearly in their interpretation of the purpose of the quotation from Is. 6 : 9f. (verse 12) in the sense of a provisional blindness and deafness.[1] Whatever other reasons they may have for this interpretation, the fact remains that, if *en parabolais* in verse 11 refers to the parables as representative for the proclamation as a whole (apart from the fact that the phrase also refers to the obscurity in which everything remains for those outside), and not as that which is intended specifically for those outside, then the purpose of the parables according to verses 11f. could not be to leave those outside in blindness and deafness.

B. The Function of Is. 6 : 9f. in Mk. 4 : 12 and Parallels

There is widespread agreement that the *hina* = "in order that" followed by a quotation from the Old Testament is an abbreviated way of saying *hina plērōthēi* = "in order that (it) may be fulfilled," which means that what follows, i.e., what is stated in the quotation, is the realization of the intention of God. So Jeremias,[2] who, however, incorrectly excludes Jesus from this intention. "The *hina*, thus, does not speak of the intention of Jesus, but of God ..."[3] The fact that the quotation expressed the intention of God, does not exclude its having been understood also as an expression of the intention of Jesus. Wilkens correctly objects against the softening of contrast which is introduced with this understanding of *hina*. "It is therefore a softening when one understands this *hina* with Jeremias ... as an abbreviation of *hina plērōthēi*. Mark is also not at all interested in scriptural truth in the manner of Matthew."[4]

Lohmeyer does not understand the *hina* in this case as an expression of the intention of God. For this he relies on the fact that,

---

[1] Jeremais, *op. cit.*, pp. (9, 11) 11f., 13; Eng. tr., pp. 15, 17; Marxsen, *op. cit.*, p. 269; Robinson, *Geschichtsverständnis*, p. 72, footnote 33; cf. below, Appendix B.

[2] *Op. cit.*, pp. (11) 13; Eng. tr., p. 17. Cf. also Lohmeyer, *op. cit.*, (cf. above p. 11, footnote 1) p. 84; Bornkamm, *mystērion*, (cf. above, p. 11, footnote 1) p. 824; Eng. tr., p. 818; Marxsen, *op. cit.*, p. 269.

[3] Jeremias, *ad loc.*

[4] *Op. cit.*, p. 311, footnote 28, cf. above, p. 11, footnote 1.

even if rarely, *hina* can mean "since" in Koine. For a discussion of this usage in the New Testament, cf. Hans Windisch, "Die Verstock-ungsidee in Mc. 4.12 und das kausale *hina* der späteren Koine,"[1] to which Lohmeyer refers. Windisch, however, rejects the causal *hina* for our text, accepting it only in the case of Apoc. 22 : 14.[2] Lohmeyer furthermore points out that Matthew (13 : 13) clearly wrote "since" (*hoti*), and that the LXX, which Mark followed, eliminated the final sense of the Hebrew of Is. 6 : 9f.[3]

Contrary to this, Bornkamm observes that the difference be-tween Matthew and Mark (also Luke) is insignificant "since all the evangelists saw in the behaviour of Jesus the fulfilment of a divine necessity laid down in scripture."[4] Marxsen follows Bornkamm in this, but apparently does not recognize the final sense of the quo-tation. "The listening not hearing is *stated* ('wird konstatiert') but in this experience the congregation sees the fulfilment of an Old Testament prophecy."[5] For Bornkamm the final sense is beyond doubt. "All the evangelists agree in (the understanding) that the parables are obscure ways of speaking and are supposed to withhold the secret of the reign of God from the people."[6] His only concession is that this "also presupposes an already existing condition with the people, which makes them ripe for the judgment of obduracy."[7]

Jeremias evades the final sense of the quotation in a different way, and is followed in this by Marxsen[8] and Robinson.[9] He interprets *mēpote* = "(in order) that not" in the quotation as "except if," following the sense of the Rabbinic exegesis of the Aramaic *dil*e*ma* in the Targum of Is. 6 : 10. He is aware that in the LXX *mēpote*, as the translation of the Hebrew *pen*, unquestionably means "(in order) that not," but is convinced that Mk. 4 : 12b is based on the Targum of Is. 6 : 10b. Thus, Mk. 4 : 12b expresses the hope that if they repent, "God will forgive them."[10] Against this it must be maintained, with Bornkamm, that "the final sense of obduracy

---

[1] *Zeitschrift für die neutestamentliche Wissenschaft*, 26 (1927), pp. 203–209.
[2] Cf. *op. cit.*, pp. 207–209.
[3] *Op. cit.*, p. 84.
[4] *Mystērion, ad loc.*
[5] *Op. cit.*, p. 269, my italicizing.
[6] *Ad loc.*
[7] *Ad loc.*
[8] *Op. cit.*, p. 269.
[9] *Geschichtsverständnis*, p. 72, footnote 33.
[10] *Op. cit.*, pp. (11, cf. 9), 13f., cf. 11f.; Eng. tr., pp. 17f., cf. 15.

should not be denied (in this saying)."[1] He is followed in this by Wilkens.[2]

C. The Parallels of Mk. 4 : 11

The only significant cases in the section with which we are concerned (Mk. 4 : 10–34, par.s), where Matthew and Luke agree with each other against Mark is in our verse and in Mt. 13 : 31–33 (cf. Lk. 13 : 18–21, which however occurs in a different context), where Matthew apparently drew from Q to expand his Markan source. In the latter section Matthew drew the following from Q: *homoia estin hē basileia tōn ouranōn* (verse 31, a verse in which he agrees with Luke against Mark, except for the *tōn ouranōn* which is an alteration he consistently makes in all his sources); *hon labōn anthrōpos* (also verse 31); *dendron* and *en tois kladois autou* (verse 32); and the addition of the entire parable of the leaven (verse 33). Matthew agrees with Mark against Luke (Q?) in the following: *mikroteron pantōn tōn spermatōn* (verse 31), and *hotan*; *meizon tōn lachanōn* and *hōste* in verse 32. In the section as a whole, i.e., Mk. 4 : 1–34 and parallels, both Matthew and Luke reveal apparent dependence on Mark.

In the first half of the saying in 13 : 11 Matthew shares *gnōnai ta mystēria*, and the word order, *hymin dedotai gnōnai ta mystēria tēs basileias*, with Luke against Mark's *hymin to mystērion dedotai tēs basileias*. In the second half of the saying, however, Matthew and Luke do not support each other against Mark in anything, and Matthew agrees with Mark against Luke with *ekeinois*, Luke agreeing with Mark against Matthew with *tois* (which, however, is a pronoun in Mark and an article in Luke), and with *en parabolais*. In this case the only word which Matthew and Luke share is *de*, which they also share with Mark. Thus, it appears that Matthew and Luke are both dependent on Mark for the second half of the saying, but the degree of agreement between them against Mark in the first half would seem to indicate some other dependence as well. This does not, of course, exclude their familiarity with the reading of the first half of the saying in Mk. 4 : 11, which both of them altered to precisely the same new reading on the basis of this other form of the saying with which they were both familiar, leaving only two

---

[1] *Jesus von Nazareth*, p. 183, note 11; Eng. tr., p. 201, note 11.
[2] *Op. cit.*, p. 311, footnote 28.

insignificant differences: Matthew's additional *hoti*, and his usual (*basileias*) *tōn ouranōn*.

The problem is how this came about. It appears improbable that in this case Matthew and Luke's agreement could be dependent on Q. It would be an extreme coincidence for both of them to have drawn together from Q only for this half verse in the entire section (Mk. 4 : 1–34 and parallels), i.e., excluding Matthew's single dependence on Q in 13 : 31–33. Wrede already suggested the two basic possibilities, i.e., either Matthew and Luke knew the saying in a form different to that of Mark, or one of them altered the Markan reading, and subsequently, but at a very early stage, the other was harmonized with it.[1]

A variation of the second possibility is the solution suggested by Wilkens. According to him, the singular *to mystērion* is the work of Mark. The original form of the saying probably had a plural *ta mystēria*, corresponding to the plural, *en parabolais*, in the second member of the antithetical parallelism.[2] However, he does not indicate whether Matthew derived the plural from this original form. He simply states: "In contrast with Mark, Matthew gives the plural *ta mystēria*."[3] Then Wilkens proceeds to identify what the plural in Matthew signifies, namely, what he refers to as the "pleophory," i.e., variety of forms of the proclamation, according to Matthew.[4] Also the *gnōnai* was introduced by Matthew, who eliminated all Mark's references to the lack of understanding of the disciples. For Matthew the *gnōnai* was given with the *dedotai* in contrast with Mark, for whom Jesus' struggle to lead the disciples to understanding was based on, but not given with the *dedotai*.[5]

This may explain very well how Matthew understood the saying, but it does not necessarily explain how he came to his altered reading. The introduction of the *gnōnai* seems very natural since there is a strong tendency in the passage to distinguish between the crowds, who remain ignorant, and the disciples. This almost calls for a reference to the understanding of the latter. However, the contrast between "those outside," who remain ignorant, and the

---

[1] *Op. cit.*, p. 62.
[2] *Op. cit.*, p. 308, footnote 13.
[3] *Op. cit.*, p. 309.
[4] *Op. cit.*, pp. 309f.
[5] *Op. cit.*, pp. 310f.; cf. footnote 23, also p. 314; cf. also Gerhard Barth, *op. cit.*, (cf. above, p. 15, footnote 3), pp. 99–104; Eng. tr., pp. 104–112.

disciples is also the point of the saying itself. Thus, it is equally possible that *gnōnai* was part of the original saying, referring to the understanding of the disciples, in contrast with the ignorance of the crowds, and that Mark eliminated the *gnōnai* because at that stage in his gospel the disciples still lacked understanding, although the secret of the Kingdom had already been given to them in contrast with the crowds. As far as the plural *ta mystēria* is concerned, Wilkens also thinks that Mark altered an original plural into the singular *to mystērion*.[1] It may be questioned, however, whether the reason which Wilkens gives for the original plural, namely, that the second plural in the antithetical parallelism of members requires it,[2] makes this conclusive.

What Wilkens does not consider is how Luke came to have a form which is verbally identical with that of Matthew only in the first half of the saying. The explanation given by Wrede, that it was harmonized at a very early stage,[3] appears improbable in view of the fact that it occurs only in this part of a verse. Thus, the other possibility suggested by Wrede[4] appears to be the preferable one, namely, that Matthew and Luke were familiar with the saying in the earlier form, i.e., in the form in which they rendered it in the first half of the parallels to Mk. 4 : 11, which does not exclude their understanding the saying in accordance with their own theology. Their support of Mark in the second half of the verse, however, seems to indicate that Mark is more original here, and that each of them altered this part of the saying in his own way without a common source different to that of Mark.

Thus, in its original form, the saying may have read: "To you it has been given to know the mysteries of the Kingdom of God, but to those who are outside everything comes in parables." Mark adapted this saying to his messianic secret motif by altering the plural *ta mystēria* into a singular, and by eliminating the *gnōnai*, which came (to the disciples) only later in the gospel. Matthew and Luke, finding no difficulty with the first half of the saying in the more primitive form in which they were familiar with it, altered it back to this earlier form, but each in his own way altered the second half of the saying, which they found incomprehensible.

---

[1] *Op. cit.*, p. 308, footnote 13.
[2] *Ad loc.*
[3] *Op. cit.*, p. 62.
[4] *Ad loc.*

TEXT INDEX

OLD TESTAMENT

NEW TESTAMENT

NON-CANONICAL PASSAGES

AUTHOR INDEX

SUBJECT INDEX

Abraham, 5, 56, 62, 73-105
  children of, filiation of, 93, 98
  "one seed" of, 79, 81, 83, 91, 96
  sonship of, 78, 80
Accidental, 90, 102
Admonition, 66f., 111
Allegorical, allegorize, allegory, 10-22, 89, 98
am ha'ares, 24, 26, 52f.
Anthropology, 36, 39, 41
Anti-historical, 81
Anti-Jewish, 94, 102
Apocalyptic, apocalypticism, 29f., 33, 68, 112
Apologetic, 42
Argument, argumentation (cf. also *reasoning*), 75, 79, 89, 103
Articulation, 23, 35, 44, 56, 59, 61f.
Ascetic, asceticism, 23, 47, 53-55
Augustus Caesar, 24
Authentic, authenticity (of tradition of Jesus—cf. also under *existence*), 4, 28, 31f., 49f., 55, 108, 113
Author(s), ix, 35, 75
Authority, 32-34, 43f., 55f.
basileia, 21
Believe (cf. also *faith*), 59, 62, 71, 88, 95, 99
Believer(s), 3, 22, 40f., 69, 81-83, 97f., 102
Brothers (cf. "*My brothers*")
Christ, 1, 3-5, 66, 69f., 72, 81f., 93, 100, 102
  concealed, 20f.
  confession of, x, 40, 62, 65f., 70-73, 105
  event, 37f., 42
  Johannine, 110
Christian(s), 9, 65, 80, 97
Christian (adj.), 1f., 33, 41f., 62, 65-67, 76f., 96f., 105
  community, 1, 20, 49, 66, 70f., 98
  condescension, 72
  early, primitive, ix, 27, 30, 37, 39f., 42
  imperialism, 72f.
Christianity, 28, 42, 56, 72
Christocentrism, 91

Christological(ly), 20, 40f., 51, 56, 59, 61, 96f., 103
Christology, 5, 20, 38f., 62, 96
  as encounter, 40f.
  explicit, 39f., 97
  functional, 97
  implied, 24f., 37, 39, 41f., 52
  indirect, 38
  Johannine, 60, 110
Church (cf. also *community*), 1, 30, 47, 51, 56, 98, 112f.
Circumcision, 88-95, 102
Claim, 1f., 5, 33, 40, 62, 78, 105
Community (cf. under *Christian*)
Conduct, 37f.
  of Jesus, 21, 25, 43, 46f., 52f.
  of John the Baptist, 47
Confession (cf. under *Christ*)
Constant, constancy, 41
Continuity, 29, 38, 99f., 103
Conversation (cf. also *dialogue*), 2
Criterion,
  of coherence, 28-32
  of discontinuity, 55
  of dissimilarity, 28-32
Cypher, 24f., 60, 105
Decision, 37, 46, 52
Definition, 90, 97f., 101f.
Descendants of Abraham (cf. also under *Abraham*), 86, 88f., 94-96
Description of the Last Judgment, 5, 56, 62, 63-73, 105
Dialogue (cf. also *conversation*), 1, 5, 73, 104
dil[e]ma, 110, 115
Disclose, 23, 32, 55f.
Discontinuity, 29-32, 55
epilysis, 107
Esau, 96
Eschatology, eschatological, 19f., 26-31, 34f., 45f., 48, 55, 81
Essential(ly), 42, 81, 83, 90, 98f., 105
Event, 2, 37f., 42, 44f., 86
Example, 62, 75, 86, 99-101
Exclusiveness, 54, 59, 105
Exhortation, 64, 68f., 71-73
Existence, 55f.
  authentic, 2f., 39f., 105